T0247108

God is... ALL *You* NEED

100 Devotions for Women

God is... ALL *You* NEED

JESSIE FIORITTO

ISBN 979-8-89151-030-2

Published by Barbour Publishing, Inc., 1810 Barbour Drive, Uhrichsville, Ohio 44683, www.barbourbooks.com

Our mission is to inspire the world with the life-changing message of the Bible.

Printed in China.

INTRODUCTION

God is all you need.

Today's women are empowered—we're CEOs and senators as well as moms, wives, and daughters. But too often we struggle under the delusion of self-sufficiency, believing we should do everything and succeed at it all. Yet after going it alone for a while, weariness takes hold. Doubt creeps in as empty places inside us begin to cry out for something better. Suddenly we realize that we need help. We need God.

Many years ago another woman felt hopeless in her helpless situation. She'd suffered for twelve long years. But then she met Jesus. Desperate, she wanted only to brush the edge of His garment with her fingertips. She knew that He had the power to change what she could not, and she was healed. Jesus told her, "Daughter, be of good comfort; your faith has healed you" (Matthew 9:22).

Open your heart to encouragement, wisdom, and strength as you explore one hundred of God's extraordinary characteristics and the ways He can fill your void with purpose and life. When you reach the end of yourself, reach out to Him. He's everything you'll ever need.

TRUTH

We are in Him who is true, even in His Son,
Jesus Christ. This is the true God and eternal life.

1 John 5:20

"One more story, please!" Three small princesses twirled around the living room, giggling in their royal bedtime finery. Eyes shining, they pleaded for just one more telling of Belle and her Beast before turning in. Snuggled into the couch and wreathed by sparkling skirts, I told them the story of a brave girl who became a princess. At the "happily ever after" my daughter sighed. "It's just like Esther."

Except. . .not quite. The Bible isn't like once upon a time. It's the truth about how God works His love story for humanity through the lives of ordinary people. And we needn't hang our hopes on the empty promises of this world, but instead on the jewels of wisdom and knowledge found in the only one who can save us. Jesus said, "If you continue in My word, then you are My disciples indeed. And you shall know the truth, and the truth shall make you free" (John 8:31–32).

Savor your time with your Savior in the pages of scripture so you're not swayed by the world's perceptions of who Jesus is. Be drawn in by His kindness and awed by His miracles. Allow His life to transform yours into one of obedience to the truth. Instead of daydreams of fairy tales, you can live in the real hope of your true happily ever after in heaven with Him.

- How have you wrestled with questions about the truth in your own life? Has your knowledge of Jesus caused you to reconsider some of your sources for truth?

- In what current life circumstances could you benefit from applying God's truth?

God, I'm thankful that Your Word is so much more than a fairy tale. Teach me to live out Your truth.

FAITHFUL

"The LORD your God, He is God, the faithful God who keeps covenant and mercy to a thousand generations with those who love Him and keep His commandments."
DEUTERONOMY 7:9

The family patriarch shuffled toward the glittering Christmas tree. Leaning heavily on his cane, he lowered himself into a chair to share the ageless telling of an uncommon baby born in a common stable. Scattered around his feet were the expectant faces of great-grandchildren, grandchildren, a daughter, a son, and a wife of many years. The serenity of his life with Jesus winked from behind kind eyes. His heart swelled with the joy of a life well lived and a family who followed in the footsteps of his faith but also with the readiness to meet his Savior.

Many years ago a graying couple reflected on their life too. . .but saw only Sarai's barrenness. Aching years passed as they lived in the expectation of a promised son. Every night Abram glanced heavenward and, seeing the countless twinkling stars, was reminded of the descendants that God had promised would ornament his family tree. "Soon," God said. And much to their laughing shock and delight, a year later they held Isaac in their arms—the covenant child whose line would bless all peoples of the earth for eternity. In His unexplainable way, God was even more faithful than we expected, not only to Abraham and Sarah but to all people who would later be saved by another baby boy of miraculous origins—a son of Abraham called Jesus.

- How does the unexpected and unexplainable way that God kept His promise to Abraham encourage, comfort, or challenge you in your life?

- How does remembering what God has done for you and others in the past give you hope in difficult times?

Lord God, You are faithful always, and nothing is too hard for You—not even my difficult circumstances.

ATONING SACRIFICE

He who did not spare His own Son but delivered Him up for us all, how shall He not also with Him freely give us all things?

ROMANS 8:32

Legs aching from the weight of the wood he carried up the steep slope, Isaac glanced at his quiet father. "Behold the fire and the wood, but where is the lamb for a burnt offering?" (Genesis 22:7). His father's slow steps halted. He glanced to heaven then met his son's questioning gaze. "My son, God will provide Himself a lamb" (Genesis 22:8).

Abraham knew Isaac was the child of promise, and if God had to raise him from the dead to keep His word, it would be so. Abraham lifted his blade. His heart pumped a sluggish beat. He clenched the handle in his shaking fist. Suddenly he heard his named called twice. Pausing, Abraham heard a command: "Do not lay your hand on the boy or do anything to him, for now I know that you fear God, seeing you have not withheld your son, your only son, from Me" (Genesis 22:12). His father's heart shuddered. His limbs trembled with sagging relief when he turned and saw the most beautiful sight. A ram caught in the brush. The lamb that would save his son.

In the fullness of time, John the Baptist's wilderness cries rang out. "Behold, the Lamb of God who takes away the sin of the world" (John 1:29). But this time, in the indrawn breath before the hammer fell, God didn't stop them. For sheer love, Jesus died in our place. And Abraham had reckoned right—this Son rose again!

- How does the knowledge that God loves you enough to die for you strengthen your relationship with Him?

- Paul wrote that we should become a living sacrifice (Romans 12:1). In what ways would becoming more sacrificial in your spiritual life benefit you?

Lord Jesus, I am overcome with gratitude for Your sacrifice. Let me live every day in joyful obedience.

LOVE

We have known and believed the love that God has for us. God is love, and he who dwells in love dwells in God, and God in him.

1 JOHN 4:16

The pain of separation had become a persistent ache, like a blister under her heel. Unexpected reminders brought fresh waves of grief for all that she'd lost. But they'd traded their tranquility for tears and toil, thistles and thorns—deceived by the serpent. For Eve and Adam, the dull throb of pain had become a squatter in their bodies and hearts. The pain snaked its way through many generations, but God could not bear to see them live forever in broken relationship with Him. The apostle Paul wrote, "The whole creation groans and labors in pain together"—but then he added two pivotal words: "until now" (Romans 8:22).

Jesus broke bread with His disciples for the final time. His words were meant to prepare them for the coming trial. They were about to witness the greatness of God's love for them. The temple veil would tear and bring their once distant relationship with God close. Jesus said, "No man has greater love than this, that a man lay down his life for his friends" (John 15:13). He knew what He was about to do—show a dying people how wide and deep is His love for us. Jesus' words to His disciples that night came with a new command. "Love one another; as I have loved you" (John 13:34). *As He loved us*—fully, unselfishly, holding nothing back. Now it's our turn.

- In what ways does knowing that God loves you so much that He would have died just for you change your life?

- Read 1 John 4:11–21. How do these verses alter your actions toward others?

Heavenly Father, You love me just because I'm Yours. Help me to love others with the same unconditional love You have shown me.

LIMITLESS

But my God shall supply all your need according to His riches in glory by Christ Jesus.

PHILIPPIANS 4:19

"I'm hungry!" Two words have never succeeded more in drawing a sigh from the lips of even the most long-suffering mother. Children have a lot of needs, most of which they can't provide for themselves. So they ask, and often demand, that we fill these voids for them. As grown-ups our needs don't vanish into our mature airs of adulthood. We too have voids, sometimes demanding ones—to be validated, to be enough, to be in control, to be liked, understood, accepted, loved, needed. . . . Our list seems endless. If you've ever been less than patient and understanding with friends, family, or coworkers who can't seem to scratch the itch of your soul's demands, you've smacked face-first into truth: people lack the capacity to fill the voids in your soul. Those empty places belong to God.

Like it or not, we humans have limits. Maybe you've had an uncomfortable encounter with the end of your resources. Maybe you yearn for acceptance or security. But, friend, in your desperation remember that God alone can satisfy all your needs and quench the desires of your aching soul. He is contained by no limits, His resources never exhausted. Philippians promises that He will supply all our needs from the riches of His glory—His limitless, infinite, never-decreasing riches. Lay aside any fear that God can't overflow your inner hollows with His boundless love, acceptance, and security.

- Is your concept of God too small for the limitless and mighty God we serve?
- How would seeing Him in a bigger and unlimited way change how you live?

God, trying to imagine the infinite reaches of all that You are makes my head ache. Help me not to turn to other people or unhealthy coping mechanisms when nothing short of You will satisfy.

GENTLE

Like a shepherd, He shall feed His flock. He shall gather the lambs with His arm and carry them in His bosom, and shall gently lead those who are with young.

Isaiah 40:11

Exhaustion hollowed her cheeks as she gently mopped her brother's burning brow. "Martha, we need Jesus." Anxious thoughts swirled in her tormented mind when the teacher remained absent. Her hope was growing as shallow as her brother's breaths. Then in a piercing twist of life's plot, Lazarus died. Why would God allow such pain to touch a family who loved Him so dearly? Their lives had been brimming with new love, new joy, and new hope. Death wasn't supposed to come calling for a brother and friend.

Instead of rushing to His friend's side, Jesus tarried two days before giving His disciples confusing words. "Lazarus is dead. And I am glad for your sakes that I was not there, so that you may believe" (John 11:14–15).

The wailing of the mourners crescendoed as Jesus approached His friend's home. His own death was darkening the horizon, and in compassion for the pain and confusion it would bring, Jesus breathed life into a gentle gift of hope for His followers when He cried out, "Lazarus, come out!" (John 11:43).

And Lazarus walked out of the tomb.

Soon, in a reckless, redemptive twist, Jesus would crush death's power forever. God hadn't written His story according to people's plan. And in the echo of this gentle preview of His resurrection, their faith would quicken and deepen until. . .

Jesus too walked out of His tomb.

So that you may believe.

- In what hidden places and unexpected circumstances might God's gentleness be revealed?

- How could recognizing God's gentleness in the midst of our pain bring you hope, comfort, and greater faith in times of hardship?

Father, life is full of confusing twists, but Your gentle hand grows my faith.

CONSUMING FIRE

That the trial of your faith, being much more precious than gold that perishes, though it is tried with fire, might be found to praise and honor and glory at the appearing of Jesus Christ.

1 PETER 1:7

She opened her eyes to darkness—and smiled. She wasn't worried. She hadn't seen the faintest flicker of light since she was six weeks old. She smiled because, although her eyes failed her, she didn't dwell in shadow. The darkness could not overcome the light of hope and joy that illuminated her soul. Instead she lived "Safe in the Arms of Jesus." Her blindness had given her spiritual sight.

Fanny Crosby, blind poet and writer of more than eight thousand hymns, said, "It seemed intended by the blessed providence of God that I should be blind all my life, and I thank him for the dispensation. If perfect earthly sight were offered me tomorrow, I would not accept it. I might not have sung hymns to the praise of God if I had been distracted by the beautiful and interesting things around me."

Job, of biblical fame, suffered soul-shattering trials as well—children dead, property destroyed, friends judging. And yet he said, "When [God] has tested me, I shall come forth as gold" (Job 23:10).

God, if we allow it, would refine us and purify us through the flames of hardship. Not to reduce us to smoldering rubble, but to exchange hope for our despair, peace for our anxiety, and joy for our depression. He would burn away the harmful distractions of sin until we are consumed by Him.

- What distractions in your life are getting in the way of God consuming your whole heart?
- Does examining how you've grown in godly character and faith through hardship change the way you view difficult circumstances?

Heavenly Father, burn away every sinful thought or distraction in my life.

IMMANUEL

"Behold, a virgin shall conceive and bear a son and shall call His name Immanuel."

ISAIAH 7:14

Her fingers were so tiny. And her bright blue gaze rested on me with such trust, and so much need. As I cradled my daughter in my arms for the first time, a troubling thought tiptoed across my mind. *Can I meet this challenge of motherhood?*

Mary must have felt flung even more out of her element. The angel had said her baby would be the Son of God. God would be. . .a baby? When labor pains knifed through her womb, she was far from home in a pungent stable with straw-encrusted sheep as her midwives. How could she mother God? She was no one great. She was no one at all really, just a scared peasant teenager. But then she touched the tiny, wrinkled fingers of God and realized that He needed her. Immanuel was just like any other baby—He needed fed and burped, changed and loved and taught. He was truly God here with us. Here in our helplessness and hunger. God had reached down with the hands of a baby to save us.

Don't worry that He won't understand your problems or that your life is too messy for the Messiah. He gets it—the financial problems, lack of status, relationship hurdles, betrayal, rejection. He's been there. He gets you. And He will absolutely be there for you. God muddied His sandals on our dusty roads so He could be with us.

- Does knowing that Jesus was God yet fully man, with the human experiences and emotions that populate our world, change your view of Him?

- How does knowing that God is right here, near you, alter the way you react in difficult situations or temptations?

God, You meet us where we are! You're here, now, with me, and You understand everything I'm going through.

SOVEREIGN

"What kind of man is this, that even the wind and the sea obey Him?"
MARK 4:41

She slammed her hand down on the SNOOZE button—again. Worry kept her walking the floor at night, but it seemed to her as if God was sleeping soundly. *Why is this happening?* One health crisis after another had stormed into her life. Her father was dying of cancer, her mother was recovering from a stroke, and her husband had just been diagnosed with a heart condition. *God, are You watching this?* she wondered.

Jesus' disciples once accused Him of sleeping on the job. They were crossing the Sea of Galilee when a storm rolled in. As fishermen, they were not likely to be intimidated by a choppy sea, but this day they believed they were destined to decorate the sea floor with another algae-covered wreck. Over the roaring wind they yelled, "Master, do You not care that we are perishing?" (Mark 4:38). Jesus' response stole the wind right out of their sails. "Peace, be still" (Mark 4:39). The howling shushed and the sea threw down its arms because the Lord God of all creation said, "Cease."

Just as the disciples did, we often forget who sails through the storms with us. Jesus asked them, "Why are you so fearful? How is it that you have no faith?" (Mark 4:40). Friend, when circumstances on your sea of life seem openly hostile, don't be afraid. Have faith that the sovereign God is still in control and can give you calm in the midst of chaos, peace instead of panic.

- In what ways does knowing that God is always with you increase your faith and peace when chaos happens?

- How can recognizing that God is the sovereign ruler over every circumstance give you comfort in difficult times?

Lord God, nothing in this world happens without Your notice. Give me courage and faith in You.

FORGIVING

"Why do you look at the speck that is in your brother's eye but do not consider the beam that is in your own eye?"

MATTHEW 7:3

Twelve men on an extended camping trip together—you have to wonder if one of his fellow disciples was dancing on his last nerve when Peter said, "Hey, Jesus, how many times do I need to forgive this guy?" He probably thought his offer of seven times was generous. But Jesus answered him, "I do not say to you, up to seven times, but up to seventy times seven" (Matthew 18:22). Sometimes we can't seem to forgive certain people once and for all. For whatever reason, offense layers over offense, and residual anger simmers.

Jesus told the story of another man who struggled to forgive. He was buried in debt, and his family was about to be sold into slavery to pay it back. But the king, moved by compassion, forgave his enormous debt. Yet instead of paying forward this unexpected generosity, the man went out and found someone who owed him far less—and had him thrown in prison. Oh, how like him we can be, when we struggle to forgive others despite our own sin debt that a lifetime of good deeds couldn't begin to repay. Yet if we ask, God forgives us over and over and over again—of every critical thought, every dishonest word and selfish action.

Beloved, you can trust Him with justice (Ecclesiastes 3:17). Because we all need forgiveness.

- How can recognizing our own faults help us to forgive others for theirs?

- In what ways does knowing that God has forgiven you of an incalculably great debt help you to forgive the offenses of others against you?

God, please forgive me for ____________ .
And I forgive ____________ for hurting me.

THE POTTER

The vessel that he made of clay was ruined in the hand of the potter. So he made it again, another vessel, as seemed good to the potter to make.

JEREMIAH 18:4

"You are that man." In a moment King David's fury faded to mourning. The prophet Nathan had told David about a rich man who'd taken a poor man's only pet lamb for his dinner. Then he laid bare David's sins of adultery and murder.

The Bible tells us that David was a man after God's own heart. These are such hopeful words because David was by no means a perfect man. But David did possess a malleable and repentant heart. He remained faithful to the God who had always been faithful to him. When he sinned, he didn't shrug his shoulders and continue doing the same thing; instead, he was deeply grieved that he'd grieved God. "Against You, You only, have I sinned, and done this evil in Your sight" (Psalm 51:4).

We are not unlike David in our propensity to sin—"we are all as an unclean thing, and all our righteousness is as filthy rags" (Isaiah 64:6). But our heavenly Father illustrates Himself as a skilled potter who specializes in remaking ruined clay into something new (Isaiah 64:8). The clay is a lifeless, uncomprehending lump of earth until the potter's hands transform it into something with both purpose and beauty. Submit your life to the Potter's hands and allow Him to shape you to be more like Jesus.

- What gap in understanding and ability lies between the lump of clay in a potter's hand and the creative plan and skill of the potter?

- How do you trust that God is shaping you in ways that seem best to Him and submit to His hand on your life?

Lord, as David prayed, create in me a clean heart and renew a right spirit in me.

OMNIPRESENT

Where shall I go from Your Spirit?
Or where shall I flee from Your presence?
Psalm 139:7

Jonah, of whale-proportioned fame, could have saved himself a boatload of trouble if he'd considered David's questions from Psalm 139:7. "Where shall I go from Your Spirit? Or where shall I flee from Your presence?" Jonah learned in a hurry that the answer to these questions is a colossal "Nowhere." There's no escaping God, and there's certainly no place you can go where God is not present. That thought is pretty incredible considering what we know about the depths of the ocean's trenches and the immeasurable vastness of the universe. Jonah certainly didn't outrun God by hopping a ship heading opposite to His plans, and neither can we.

David continued with his thoughts on the situation: "If I ascend up into heaven, You are there. If I make my bed in hell, behold, You are there" (Psalm 139:8). That pretty much covers it. God is everywhere that you will ever be.

If you feel that you've pitched your tent in a godforsaken place, He is there. Take comfort in knowing that He is with you through depression, hardship, disappointments, failures, and weaknesses. If your emotions are telling you that God has deserted you, cling to the clear truth that God is with you always. If your sins have opened a spiritual chasm between you and God, return to Him, and He will show you His infinite compassion and forgiveness (Isaiah 55:6–7).

- Does God's omnipresence encourage or frighten you? Why?

- Think about a difficult situation you were in recently. How would remembering God's omnipresence have helped you?

> *God, I praise You that I can't escape You.*
> *No matter where I go You are already there.*

OMNISCIENT

There is no creature that is not known in His sight.
HEBREWS 4:13

"Surprise!" My sister managed to throw an amazing sweet-sixteen birthday party for my niece. My sister is apparently a miracle worker, because the look on her daughter's face when she opened the door to fifty of her friends and family said it all—she was in total shock.

As awesome as her party was, I'm so thankful that God never looks at my life and says, "Wow, didn't see that one coming." God is never surprised or caught off guard by anything that enters our lives. He even knows the number of hairs on your head (Matthew 10:30). There's nothing He isn't privy to. And that means the God who created you knows everything about you. No thought, emotion, or action escapes His notice. David understood this wonderful truth when he penned, "O LORD, You have searched me and known me. You know when I sit down and when I rise up; You understand my thought from afar" (Psalm 139:1–2).

David was awestruck by the ramifications of God's omniscience over his life. Anxiety-inducing situations caused less worry. Goliath-sized obstacles shrank when compared to God. And the image of God monitoring our thoughts will surely help purify our inner dialogue and swipe some of sin's seductiveness. "Such knowledge is too wonderful for me" (Psalm 139:6).

Be at peace because nothing can surprise God. He bought you with the blood of Christ, and He won't return you because an old skeleton rattles in your closet. He knew everything there was to know before He paid the price.

- What does God know about us, and what can we learn about God from this?

- In what ways does God's omniscience affect your life?

Heavenly Father, nothing in my past is a shock to You, and You love me and forgive me in spite of knowing it all.

JEALOUS

"I have redeemed you. I have called you by your name. You are Mine."

ISAIAH 43:1

Tent flaps rustled in the stiff morning breeze as thunder rolled over the hills. Fingers of smoke wrapped Mount Sinai in haze. God had come to the mountain. Moses left the Israelites camped at its base and climbed the craggy heights to speak with God. Little did he know that the restless Israelites were already breaking the first command God had inscribed into the stone tablets: "You shall have no other gods before Me" (Exodus 20:3). God had miraculously freed them from slavery, and yet they strayed. They demanded a golden calf. Oh, how inconstant our hearts can be.

How often we're like the Israelites—overeager to sell our souls and bodies back into sin, whether we're trapped in addiction, struggling to forgive, or prioritizing our careers, pleasures, or social lives over God. But God still lays claim to our affections: "I have redeemed you. I have called you by your name. You are Mine" (Isaiah 43:1).

If you fear that you're too deeply wrapped in sin, take hope. God has freed you from all sins. You belong to Him. He's jealous for your love because the one who formed you loves you best. Paul told the Corinthian church, "I am jealous for you with godly jealousy. For I have betrothed you to one husband, that I may present you as a chaste virgin to Christ" (2 Corinthians 11:2). Jesus sacrificed Himself for you to prove His true love. He will cherish you forever. So stay with Him. Be faithful to the true lover of your soul.

- What does it mean that God is jealous, and what implications does it have for our personal behavior?

- How does God's jealousy reflect His love for us?

Lord, You are forever kind and good.
I will not be wooed by worldly things.

THE DOOR

"Truly, truly, I say to you, I am the door of the sheep."
JOHN 10:7

Thanks to one of my homeschool-mom "oh my goodness my kids need fire safety training" moments, my girls discovered a new "door" to the front porch. They are now escape masters who take every opportunity to trip the lock, shove open the sash, and boost each other to freedom through this fascinating portal. Because of their newfound safety consciousness, my husband now makes nightly rounds, checking all the downstairs windows and making sure everything is secure for the night. Then he kisses them and tells them to sleep tight because everything is buttoned up.

Jesus said that He was the good shepherd and the door of the sheep. In Israel shepherds built sheepfolds out of stones to protect their sheep at night. In the evening the shepherd would gather his sheep into the pen and camp out in the entrance. He was, quite literally, the door. Nothing could get to his sheep without coming through him.

Today's world teems with anxiety-inducing change and circumstances. But God watches over your life. He is the door. Nothing will touch your life that hasn't been filtered through His faithful fingers. Hard things will come—a cancer diagnosis, a divorce, a wayward child. But God is sovereign over all His creation. The God who has the power to raise kingdoms and calm violent storms loves you and works all things together for good for those who love Him and are called according to His purpose (Romans 8:28).

- What is the significance of Jesus' "I am the door" statement?

- What comfort and implications does this verse hold for your life?

Father, this world isn't spinning out of control even if my circumstances feel chaotic. I know that You watch over me.

TEACHER

"Take My yoke on you and learn from Me,
for I am meek and lowly in heart."
Matthew 11:29

The farmer laughed at the shenanigans of his young ox. It bellowed in protest as it kicked and grunted, twisting sharply in the new yoke. It darted forward and dug in its heels in turns only to come against the patient plodding and brute force of the older, experienced ox that was tasked with teaching this young rebel some manners. The farmer knew if he was going to get any work out of this stubborn animal, it would have to learn to yield to the yoke, to pull together with its partner.

Jesus invites us to be yoked to Him so we can learn from His steps. With the same humility that had Him stepping out of heaven and into our immature and foolish lives, He is willing to yoke Himself to even exasperating children. He's a gentle teacher. Never harsh. Not easily frustrated or angered. He gently and patiently schools us in the actions of love.

Jesus promises that His yoke is easy and that He won't lay anything heavy on us. The more mature ox patiently plods along, carrying the majority of the load. Jesus is big enough to carry the load too. We just need to keep in step with Him.

But at times we run ahead and exhaust ourselves or lag behind because we don't really like where Jesus is taking us. Beloved, watch how Jesus walks. Walk like He does and keep in step with the Spirit. Yield to His yoke.

- Jesus calls Himself meek and lowly in heart. In what ways does this comfort you and challenge your perceptions of Him?

- How do Jesus' gentleness and lowliness of heart invite you into knowing Him more deeply?

Lord, You are a patient and gentle teacher. Help me to learn Your ways so I can participate in Your plans.

PEACE

Be anxious for nothing.
PHILIPPIANS 4:6

Anxiety is like a sudden drop in barometric pressure. A frigid gust on a sunny day. It sends tremors sheeting down your spine that steal your breath and stab tension between your shoulders. It's a thunderhead blotting a clear horizon that also clouds your thoughts and floods your mind with uneasiness, leaving you shaking, sweaty, and sleepless. The words *what if* rumble on a loop through your mind. It's less the fear of what *will* happen and more the paralyzing gloom of what *might* happen.

If you've become a reclusive Negative Nancy, living with permanent frown lines under a sky that's always falling, God has words of hope for you:

> *Rejoice in the Lord always, and again I say, rejoice. Let your moderation be known to all men. The Lord is at hand. Be anxious for nothing, but in everything, by prayer and supplication with thanksgiving, let your requests be made known to God. And the peace of God, which passes all understanding, shall guard your hearts and minds through Christ Jesus. Finally, brothers, whatever things are true, whatever things are*

honest, whatever things are just, whatever things are pure, whatever things are lovely, whatever things are of good report, if there is any virtue, and if there is any praise, think on these things.

PHILIPPIANS 4:4–8

Let His truth ease the knots of tension from your tired body. God is good. He is in control. He is with you, all the time. There's joy in that truth. Hand Him your concerns, and laser-focus your mind on the good things. You'll discover His soothing peace of mind.

- In what ways can our anxiety lead us into sin?
- How could you reframe anxious thoughts to rejoice in the Lord and find courage in light of God's goodness and sovereignty?

Lord, my Prince of Peace,
I need Your calm in my storms.

BEAUTIFUL

One thing I have asked of the Lord, *that I will seek after: that I may dwell in the house of the* Lord *all the days of my life, to behold the beauty of the* Lord *and to inquire in His temple.*

Psalm 27:4

The woods were on fire, and she couldn't drag her eyes from the beauty of it. The fall foliage was aflame with rich crimson and burnished gold. The perfection of nature was both irresistible and attractive. The beauty of creation brought to her mind the beauty of its Creator. Saint Augustine wrote, "You, Lord, who are beautiful made them for they are beautiful. . . . You are, for they are."

Maybe *beautiful* isn't the first word that comes to your mind when you think of God, but the attractiveness of His creation is merely a dull reflection of God's beauty. Because He is beautiful, His creation has no choice but to be beautiful. God's beauty isn't bound by what we can see, but it radiates from His perfect character.

Masterfully magnetic, exquisite in its composition, fascinating in its perfection—that is the image of God's beauty. God is beautiful because He is excellent. His perfect character shines attractive light into our dark world because He possesses all that is desirable. He promised, "Your eyes shall see the King in His beauty" (Isaiah 33:17). And then He unveiled His glory in the face of Jesus (2 Corinthians 4:6). His appearance wasn't striking, but God's bright glory shone in the beautiful actions of Jesus.

- What is God's beauty?
- If we go looking for God's beauty in scripture and creation, where can we find it?

God, You are glorious perfection.
I, like David, want to dwell with
You and see Your beauty all my life.

HOLY

Who is like You, glorious in holiness,
fearful in praises, doing wonders?
Exodus 15:11

Hope had faded to a distant pinprick of light in her darkness. She felt dirty, unworthy. The things that she'd done. . . Her sins certainly stood between her and God. She knew that He was holy, perfect, unsoiled by the kind of crippling shame she felt. Like the Israelites she'd heard about as a child, she did evil in the sight of God. And again, she did evil in the sight of God. And again. . .

Centuries ago the prophet Isaiah had a vision. He was in the throne room of God. The foundations of the smoky room shook with the Lord's voice. The seraphim called out, "Holy, holy, holy, is the Lord of hosts. The whole earth is full of His glory" (Isaiah 6:3). Isaiah too was overwhelmed by his unworthiness and feared he would be struck dead in the violent reaction when God's holiness rejected his sin like water exploding from a pan of hot grease: "Woe is me! . . . I am a man of unclean lips," he cried (Isaiah 6:5). But instead of condemnation he saw the grace of God. The seraphim removed a hot coal from the altar and touched it to his lips: "Your guilt is taken away, and your sin purged" (Isaiah 6:7).

All our guilt is gone! We're forgiven. Beloved, go and sin no more.

- In what ways does it change your life that Jesus gave His life to take away your guilt, to forgive your sins and pay your debt?

- Do you have habits in your life that you need to stop, or perhaps start?

God, the scouring brightness of Your holiness is a fearsome sight. Thank You for Jesus. Give me strength to resist temptation and live for You.

RESCUER

Lord, how long will You look on? Rescue my soul from their destructions, my dear life from the lions.

PSALM 35:17

Her son lay in the hospital bed, monitors beeping, tubes crawling across his frail frame. Double pneumonia had spread faster than the doctors had ever seen, and now he lay clinging to a thread of life. She gripped her faith in a white-knuckled fist. Under her skin a tremor began. Anxiety set in. What if. . . God didn't rescue her from this?

Another young boy once lay in unexpectedly dire circumstances. Stuck at the bottom of a well, Joseph screamed for his murderous brothers to lift him out, but that was only the prelude to his nightmare. Sold into slavery, he was slandered and shoved into prison—forgotten. Or so it seemed.

But God was working. In His infinite knowledge He'd set the pieces for checkmate. God never left Joseph. And He's with us too. His plans are good. No, not every situation is good. Sickness is not good. Slavery, false accusations, and prison are not good. But God can blend all the elements together and render evil into good. As Joseph told his astounded brothers, "You thought evil against me, but God meant it for good, to bring to pass, as it is this day, to save many people alive" (Genesis 50:20). And God's incredible rescue plan stretched to reach us all through His ultimate checkmate against evil—Jesus.

- Reflect on a time when God rescued you *from* something bad. In what ways has He rescued you *through* hard circumstances that make sense only in hindsight?

- In what ways does the example of Joseph's life help you to trust in God's goodness and sovereignty?

God, I am rescued in Christ! And even when I don't fully understand, I know You are with me, working for my good.

HUMBLE

Being found in appearance as a man,
He humbled Himself and became obedient
to death, even the death of the cross.
PHILIPPIANS 2:8

The wicked gleam in his eye forecast rough waters for both my brother and my husband. My dad loves boating, and towing people on the tube tickles him with special joy. Personally, I believe he's working in his way to improve our prayer lives as we beg God's mercy for our stupidity and hubris in thinking we can tame his "fun." I know because I've sent out a few terror-stricken pleas while white-knuckling the flimsy plastic handles of a vinyl doughnut, beaten by the chop at twenty-five miles an hour. That morning the young guys had been crowing their invincibility. So when Dad winked at me and flipped his hat around backward, I took a firm grip on the rail, because I knew he was preparing to shred their sails—and I was praying that we'd end our day with safe harbor and not screaming sirens.

God can certainly use difficult circumstances to humble us, but our heavenly Father doesn't have a wicked desire to see us crushed. Instead His fierce love for us fuels His desire that we would know the abundance of a life fully submitted to Him. Jesus stepped into our den of disobedience and self-importance in the form of a servant. He said, "Blessed are the meek, for they shall inherit the earth" (Matthew 5:5). The humble—the gentle souls who don't shove others aside and force results in life to further their own agendas—will inherit everything. Instead of putting yourself forward, serve others in love, and trust God for the outcome.

- In what ways do you need to nurture a servant's heart toward both God and other people?

- When have you experienced a humbling event that brought you closer to God?

Lord, teach me to value others above myself.

BRIDEGROOM

"I will betroth you to Me forever. Yes, I will betroth you to Me in righteousness and in judgment and in loving-kindness and in mercies. I will even betroth you to Me in faithfulness. And you shall know the LORD."

HOSEA 2:19–20

Sweat traced the tired planes of his face. Anticipation added a swift economy to his movements as he heaved his nail gun one last time and fixed the final piece of molding in place. He'd designed this house for the one he loved. A smile pulled at the corner of his mouth. Laughter would soon christen the halls of this house. . .no, this home.

Another carpenter once wore calluses into strong hands. It's somehow fitting that the Creator of the world built useful things with the needs and delight of His people in mind. On the night before His death, Jesus sensed His disciples' distress and laid aside His own private agony to reassure them, and us. "In my Father's house are many mansions; if it were not so, I would have told you. I go to prepare a place for you. . . . I will come again and receive you to Myself, that where I am, there you may be also" (John 14:2–3).

Imagine the lover of your soul, the one who gave Himself up to make you holy and blameless (Ephesians 5:25–26), taking your hand to show you what He's built. . .a forever home filled with love and joy. Be ready, beautiful bride of Christ. He's coming soon!

- How does the anticipation of your future home with Christ give you strength and hope in the hardships of this life?

- Reflect on Revelation 19:6–9. In what ways might Jesus be working to purify and beautify His church, His bride?

Lord, may I be found faithful and waiting when You return for Your bride.

GOOD

O taste and see that the LORD is good.
PSALM 34:8

BROTHER KILLS BROTHER IN JEALOUS RAGE. We've been trying to make sense of life's devastation since the first couple was evicted from paradise only to wake up to this horrifying headline. Many of us question how God can be so good when bad things keep happening.

The apostle Paul understood hardship. He wrote that he was

> *more abundant in labors, above measure in beatings, more frequent in prisons, often near death. Five times I received from the Jews forty lashes less one. Three times I was beaten with rods. Once I was stoned. Three times I endured shipwreck. A night and a day I have been in the deep. I have been on journeys often, in peril from waters, in peril from robbers, in peril by my own countrymen, in peril by the Gentiles, in peril in the city, in peril in the wilderness, in peril in the sea, in peril among false brothers, in weariness and painfulness, often in sleepless nights,*

in hunger and thirst, in fasting often, in cold and nakedness. Besides those external things, those that come on me daily—the concern for all the churches.

2 Corinthians 11:23–28

Yes, Paul had felt the bite of pain. Yet this is the same man who wrote, "Rejoice in the Lord always" (Philippians 4:4). So what's his secret? Paul knew that an infinitely good God can produce something good and precious in us through our trials—a fully mature faith.

- How have you experienced God's goodness in your life? In what situations or circumstances do you struggle to believe that God is good to you?

- In God's good plan even our trials are part of the process of preparing us for glory. What seems hard to accept about that? What's comforting about it?

God, I trust that You will bring good from bad. Amen.

ETERNAL

Now to the King eternal, immortal, invisible, the only wise God, be honor and glory forever and ever. Amen.

1 Timothy 1:17

"Last one to the pond is a rotten egg!" Childhood summers seem to stretch on forever. As kids, my sister and I unfurled our towels on the dock and soaked in the lazy heat before leaping into the cool waters of our pond. Time meandered while we floated circles on old tire tubes. We lived by the creed "Don't worry about yesterday or tomorrow; just be."

When Moses met God, he asked Him the same thing many of us probably would have—His name. And God said, "I Am That I Am." No birth date recorded. No ending in sight. Just I Am. As He has always been.

As much as our summers felt eternal, our days are numbered. We are mortal and will fade like the flowers in fall. "For we will surely die and be as water spilled on the ground, which cannot be gathered up again. . . . Yet He devises plans that His banished ones are not expelled from Him" (2 Samuel 14:14). Our lives are barely a blink when compared to the eternal God who loves us. And His plan for us is Jesus.

Paul challenged us to gaze "not at the things that are seen, but at the things that are not seen. For the things that are seen are temporal, but the things that are not seen are eternal" (2 Corinthians 4:18). Jesus alone can give us the precious, invisible gift of eternal life. And the more I dwell on the promise of heaven, the more precious He becomes.

- According to John 3:16, John 17:3, and Romans 6:23, what is eternal life?

- How does having eternal life affect your life now?

Heavenly Father, help me to be just, to love kindness, and to walk humbly with You forever (Micah 6:8).

MESSIAH

"The Spirit of the Lord is upon Me, because He has anointed Me to preach the gospel to the poor. He has sent Me to heal the brokenhearted, to preach deliverance to the captives, and recovery of sight to the blind, to set at liberty those who are bruised, to preach the acceptable year of the Lord."

LUKE 4:18–19

He wasn't at all what they were expecting. "Isn't that Mary and Joseph's son. . .the carpenter? Doesn't His sister live down the street?" Jesus went to the Nazareth synagogue and read Isaiah's prophecy of the coming Messiah. He told His friends, family, and neighbors, "Today this scripture is fulfilled in your ears" (Luke 4:21). Their rejection was so violent that they tried to kill Him, but God said, "Not yet." So Jesus walked right through the crowd.

Sometimes God isn't what we were expecting in our lives either. Sometimes we reject His gentle voice: "Forgive. Calm your pride. Help your neighbor. Love your enemy." Many people rejected Jesus because He wasn't their ideal Messiah. They wanted revolution. He gave them redemption. They wanted a king. He gave them a carpenter. They wanted prestige. He gave them peace. They wanted a lion. God sent them His perfect lamb.

God did the unexpected and gave us what we never imagined possible. He gave us grace. "His own did not receive Him. But as many as received Him, to them He gave power to become the sons of God, even to those who believe in His name" (John 1:11–12). His suffering saved us all.

- Why were the Jewish people so skeptical of Jesus' claim to be the Messiah?

- Do you ever reject Jesus when He doesn't act as you would have Him in your life?

God, Jesus may not be the Savior
we expected, but He's the one we need.
Thank You for being so unlike us!

BLESSING

Blessed is the God and Father of our Lord Jesus Christ, who has blessed us with all spiritual blessings in the heavenly places in Christ.

EPHESIANS 1:3

Their bodies ached from the merciless beating they'd received from the city authorities. Their stomachs were hollow with hunger, and their throats were as dry as the dusty roads they'd walked to Philippi. Comfort was a prize held just out of reach by the stocks that bound them to the prison floor. In the midst of this agonizing miscarriage of justice, "at midnight Paul and Silas were praying and singing praises to God" (Acts 16:25).

How. . .unexpected. The jailer and the other prisoners must have been confused by their response. Or maybe they questioned their sanity. What were they singing about? Who were they praying to, and why the joy? As an added blessing, after a reality-shaking earthquake, the jailer asked Paul, "What must I do to be saved?" (Acts 16:30). That night he and his whole family became believers in the Blessing.

Paul and Silas knew that even on our worst days we're still living in the blessings of God. Don't let a bad day, a hard circumstance, or a failure steal the joy you have in knowing, without a doubt, that God is right there with you. We're saturated in blessings. We just have to see them. A new day will dawn. You're still breathing in and out. And Jesus still died to save you. Let this reality be the lens through which you view this moment, this day, this year, this life.

- Have you ever responded in an unexpectedly gracious way to hardship or injustice that made others curious about Jesus?
- Which blessings of God help you most to respond with prayer and praise in difficult situations?

God, You've blessed me extravagantly. Even if I have nothing on this earth, You died for me.

PROVIDER

"Therefore do not worry, saying, 'What shall we eat?' or 'What shall we drink?' or 'With what shall we be clothed?' . . . For your heavenly Father knows that you have need of all these things."

MATTHEW 6:31–32

My husband will not allow me to pack the car when we travel to visit my parents. Apparently I lack the ability to stack our luggage like Tetris blocks and am severely optimistic that my parents possess such basic needs as soap, towels, and pillows. From work boots to house slippers, we're strapped in like the Clampetts headed to Beverly Hills. We may not have packed the kitchen sink, but not to worry: we have a jumbo tub of wet wipes in case a Vesuvius of chocolate milk erupts in the back seat. Often we like to MacGyver our spiritual lives in this way too. We're prepared for every contingency. We've got this, God. . .until we don't.

The huge crowds that gathered to hear Jesus teach didn't have my husband as their travel coordinator. They hadn't brought their U-Hauls or even a picnic basket. Now evening was setting in and everyone was getting a bit hangry, including the disciples, who were ready to send the crowds packing. Just when everyone was on the brink of exasperation,

Andrew dragged one Boy Scout to Jesus; maybe he was a distant cousin of my husband. You can almost hear the disciples roll their eyes at his lunch box. But they'd forgotten who they were dining with. Jesus took the bread and fish, thanked His Father, and fed them—every last person.

- In what ways does your perspective on the problems you face change when you remember that you're with Jesus?
- What seemingly insurmountable needs or struggles will you trust Jesus with today?

Heavenly Father, thank You for providing what I need. Give me greater faith and wipe out my worry.

WISE

Incline your ear to wisdom and apply
your heart to understanding.
PROVERBS 2:2

You're a fool, she thought. She trudged along, her muscles straining under the weight of heavy water jars. Sweat dampened her clothes, and the sun glared at her from directly overhead as if it too mocked her. Yet another foolish choice in a long list of mistakes that seemed to define her life. She hauled water in the heat of the day to avoid the snide laughter and cold stares of the other women. But today someone was waiting for her by the well. Another man to bring trouble into her life, no doubt. And this man *did* list all her mistakes—but He disarmed her completely with grace instead of condemnation.

We can't hide our shame or foolishness from God. But He wants so much more for us than to be defined by our mess-ups. The Bible says, "If any of you lacks wisdom, let him ask of God, who gives to all men generously and without reproach, and it shall be given him" (James 1:5). You're just an ask away from His infinite wisdom.

How do you connect with your kids when they're distant? What should you prioritize in your life? Should you take that new job offer? How do you forgive someone who has hurt you? Ask Him. Like the Samaritan woman, if you truly realized who you were asking, you would ask and He would give you so much more than you realized you needed.

- How has foolishness (selfishness, pride, anger, presumption, and the like) affected your life or the lives of people you know?

- What does it take to be a person of wisdom, and what would you say is the difference between a moral duty to wisdom and a grace-filled invitation to wisdom?

Lord, please fill me with Your wisdom when dealing with __________________________.

BREATH OF LIFE

"The Spirit of God has made me, and the breath of the Almighty has given me life."
Job 33:4

"She's not breathing!" My mind was in shock as I performed CPR on my nine-month-old daughter. I compressed her chest with two fingers and watched her lips fade to blue. "Just breathe," I prayed. "Please, God. Just let her breathe." Just as the EMTs burst through our front door my daughter gasped and her chest expanded as she pulled life-preserving oxygen into her lungs. We learned at the hospital that she'd had a breath-holding spell. Usually brought on by fear or pain, a forced exhale steals their breath for a few seconds to over a minute before they inhale. Her episodes always left me a little shaken, but less so after we knew they weren't harmful. Finally, around three years old, she grew out of it. My husband dubbed her our little fainting goat.

We breathe around twenty-two thousand times each day without a thought for the precious, life-sustaining process. In the Bible breath represents God's Spirit. Breathe. Breathe deeply. And with every breath be reminded of God's presence—His Holy Spirit that dwells in every believer.

Psalm 139:8 offers this comfort: "If I ascend up into

heaven, You are there. If I make my bed in hell, behold, You are there." No matter the heights of joy or the depths of struggle you find yourself in, God is there with you. He's sovereign. He loves you. In your scary moment the steadying hand of the Holy Spirit was holding us. Even if things had turned out differently, God is still good. He's there with you too.

- What does it mean to receive the breath of life, and what comfort does His presence bring in your daily life?

- Where can you see the Holy Spirit working in your life and in the world?

Father God, You breathed out a precious gift upon us—Your power and presence.

CREATOR

Have you not known? Have you not heard that the everlasting God, the LORD, the Creator of the ends of the earth, does not lose strength, nor is weary? There is no searching of His understanding.

ISAIAH 40:28

My grandmother was nearly miraculous at feeding people. Raised during scarce times, she'd perfected the talent for using everything available to its fullest potential. Her door was always open, and when friends stopped by, a plate of cookies or a pineapple upside-down cake seemed to materialize out of thin air.

Let's turn back time for a moment—all the way back to the first blaze of dawn on the horizon. As talented a cook as my grandmother was, she still required some flour, lard, and buttermilk to bake a batch of biscuits. God, however, is in a category far above my grandma. He started with nothing. Without the aid of raw materials or preexisting matter, He created every electron, atom, and molecule, each grain of silky sand, thunderous ocean wave, and blushing sunset. Towering cedars and fragrant lilacs, the delicate lace of a butterfly's wings and the lion's raw power—they're all credited to His artistic genius. He alone is our magnificent Creator who can bring something into being with merely the command of His voice (Genesis 1:3).

And the crowning achievement of His creation is you. "Let Us make man in Our image, according to Our likeness" (Genesis 1:26). He creates because He loves, and He loves us because we are His.

- What part of the creation story draws you closer to God?

- God created you in His image and wants a relationship with you. In what ways does this knowledge shape your life?

God, You are the master designer of the universe. And yet You crave a relationship with me enough to die so that I could be with You. Thank You.

LIFE

Jesus said to him, "I am the way, the truth, and the life."
John 14:6

"What have I done?"

Oh, how often we find ourselves in Eve's shoes. Stung by sin, reflecting with regret over actions we're desperate to take back. Too late we realize that sinful behavior is not benevolent. It doesn't add anything to the fullness of our joy. Instead, like Satan, it kills our relationships, steals our joy, and destroys our lives. We can't undo our mess, but there's someone who can remove the stain and take us from death into life again.

Jesus came that we might have life and have it abundantly (John 10:10). God Himself is life. He is vibrant. He breathed into Adam; and full, bountiful life is what He intends for us. Satan tried to split us up; but praise God that He was never satisfied with being separated from us. Instead of walking away from ungrateful creatures gone awry, God the Father sent a Savior to restore us to life. "God has given to us eternal life, and this life is in His Son. He who has the Son has life, and he who does not have the Son of God does not have life" (1 John 5:11–12).

Beloved, that life begins now! Throw off your wretched, lifeless habits and come to the Son who died so you could live. Follow His way, live by His truth, and receive His life, rich in meaning, spilling over with joy, and lavish with eternal blessings.

- Consider John 3:16. Have you believed in the sacrificial death of Jesus that gives new life?
- What sins have you allowed to reside in your life that are stealing the abundance and meaning from your life in Christ?

God, You are life—full, vivacious, satisfying life that never fades. For a thousand years and then ten thousand more I want to live to the highest potential.

ABLE

To Him who is able to do exceedingly abundantly above all that we ask or think, according to the power that works in us, to Him be glory.

EPHESIANS 3:20–21

The brake pedal sank to the floorboards with a grinding scrape. My husband has many wonderful talents, but a mechanic he is not. When his brakes went out, he could have had an accident or been without transportation for days. But it just so happened—or rather God happened—that he broke down right in front of a mechanic's garage. And God also happened to know that said mechanic was in need of a little extra work. He worked into the night to fix my husband's brakes in one day. Praise God for seeing to everyone's needs!

God is able to do anything He wishes. And with our God all things are possible (Matthew 19:26). He can bend our bad into blessings if we keep walking with Him through the wreck. God asked Abraham, "Is anything too hard for the LORD?" (Genesis 18:14). And Abraham knew the answer is a resounding "No!" when Isaac was born long after their hope of a child was dead.

God is able to work wonders in our lives when we surrender to His plans as Jesus did: "Not My will, but Yours, be done" (Luke 22:42). God's ability is not limited by our disability either. When we recognize our own weakness (2 Corinthians 12:8–10) and trust solely in God's ability, He shows up for us.

- What hardships are you facing? How can you develop unshakable trust in God, including when He doesn't save you from difficult circumstances?

- When was a time you followed God despite your weakness so the strength of God could be seen? How did He show up?

Lord God, You are able! I know and trust that nothing is too hard for You.

FATHER

If you endure chastening, God deals with you as with sons, for what son is he whom the father does not chasten?
HEBREWS 12:7

I could have died. I'd messed up in a major way. The anticipation of the discipline headed my way seemed more agonizing than the punishment. My siblings and I were young but old enough to know better. One toe on the ice of our pond turned into a foot and then two. Soon we were sliding out toward the middle—without our parents' permission. Our tracks on the pond scared several years off my dad's life. And our lives were essentially over for several weeks after that. It was a painful punishment for a dangerous sin. My father's discipline was driven by love and his desire never to see us in such danger again.

Sin is real. And it is deadly. But, sometimes to our dismay, we have a loving heavenly Father who steps in to correct us when our wrong actions endanger us. "My son, do not despise the discipline of the LORD or be weary of His correction. For those whom the LORD loves, He corrects, like a father with the son in whom he delights" (Proverbs 3:11–12).

Failing to turn children from the error of their ways is not love. He corrects, not because He is angry or disappointed, but because His intense love will not permit Him to be indifferent to what's best for His children.

- What does Psalm 51 teach us about heeding God's discipline and nurturing a humble and repentant heart?

- What encouragement can you find in God's hand of discipline on your life (Hebrews 12:5–11)?

Heavenly Father, I don't always like to be corrected. But I'm thankful that You love me too much to leave me to my sins. Create a clean heart in me.

PLEDGE OF OUR INHERITANCE

After you believed you were sealed with the Holy Spirit of promise, who is the guarantee of our inheritance until the redemption of the purchased possession, to the praise of His glory.

EPHESIANS 1:13–14

Her steps echoed in the empty hall of her parents' house. The spark of life had fled since they'd died. Memories stirred as she wandered through the rooms cleaning out all the closets and shelves that held the leftovers of their life. She'd also uncovered her mom's secret habit—she kept everything. Receipts from thirty years before. Boxes of unlabeled pictures that had obviously meant something to her parents, but she didn't recognize the nameless faces smiling out from the prints. The garage was filled with gadgets and tools she had no idea how to use. She smiled at the reminders of their life, but she knew these things were not her true inheritance.

In ancient times when land was sold, the seller would give a soil sample to the buyer as a pledge of what was promised. God has given us His pledge too—the Holy Spirit is our guarantee that His promises will be fulfilled. "For all the promises of God are yes in Him. . .who has also sealed us and given the Spirit in our hearts as a guarantee" (2 Corinthians 1:20, 22).

God's promises are all yes in Jesus! Don't store treasures here in this broken place. Focus on your heavenly inheritance that is imperishable, undefiled, and unfading (1 Peter 1:4).

- What spiritual things do we inherit as children of God?

- In what areas of your life do you need to shift to a mindset of heavenly inheritance?

Heavenly Father, we're living in the "not yet" of Your promises, but thank You for giving us a pledge and a foretaste of the glory to come.

SELF-SUFFICIENT

"God, who made the world and all things in it, seeing that He is Lord of heaven and earth, does not dwell in temples made with hands. Nor is He worshipped with men's hands, as though He needed anything."

Acts 17:24–25

I'd missed the explosion. Pancake batter dripped from the counter and stove and streaked my daughter's glowing face. Deformed pancakes were stacked in a lopsided pile—their condition ranged from charred to gooey. She perched on a chair in front of the stove and wielded her spatula like a scepter. "I made breakfast, Mom!"

God is complete in Himself and dependent on His creation for nothing. But this attribute belongs to Him alone. When we go our own way, never seeking God, we often realize that the masterpiece we were after has become our mess. The prophet Jeremiah pleaded with Israel to return to God, but they responded, "We will walk according to our own plans, and everyone will do the plans of his evil heart" (Jeremiah 18:12). Culture sells us the lie "You are enough." But the truth is that we are not and will never be enough. We need God.

And He does cherish us. But we aren't valuable to Him

because He needs anything from us. We're precious to Him because He made us and loves us. This is great news! We never have to worry that God keeps us around only because we're useful to Him and that He'll drop us when we're not. Our salvation is not dependent on anything we can do. He saved us because He loves us.

- In what ways have you tried to be self-sufficient and left God out of your decisions? What were the results?

- After reading Acts 17:22–34, what comfort and hope can we have knowing that God doesn't depend on us?

> *God, I need You in my life. I'm so thankful that I don't have to make it on my own.*

PATIENCE

Rest in the Lord, *and wait patiently for Him. Do not fret because of him who prospers in his way, because of the man who brings wicked schemes to pass.*

Psalm 37:7

She wasn't the first woman to think that God needed a little push from her to get His job done, and she certainly wasn't the last. Sarai had waited years for a promised son. Maybe she and Abram had misunderstood. So Sarai devised a plan to help.

Sometimes we can't wait for God's timing and we step all over His toes with our out-of-sync moves as we question His intentions, His love, and His plan. Why do injustices go unpunished? Why do evil people prosper? Why do loved ones continue to make destructive choices? Why doesn't God put a stop to it now?

Years later Sarai's great-grandson probably pondered these same questions while he sat in prison waiting for God to move on his behalf. But eventually Joseph was uniquely positioned to save his family from starvation. "The Lord is not slow concerning His promise, as some men count slowness, but is long-suffering toward us, not willing that any should perish but that all should come to repentance" (2 Peter

3:9). Joseph could have believed his life had been derailed by a series of calamities; but he trusted God. Instead of a train wreck he was on track for God's greater plan.

- Have you ever experienced a situation where you've struggled to trust God for the outcome or tried to take control of the situation yourself? What was the result?

- Why is it hard to be patient when you are suffering or in pain, and what response do you have in this situation? In what ways does knowing that God is near comfort you (Philippians 4:5)?

Father, forgive me for rushing in when I should wait for You. Fill me with hope and peace in the waiting.

PERSONAL

"I have called you friends, for all things that I have heard from My Father I have made known to you."
JOHN 15:15

He wiped the sweat from his face and hurried through the streets to his booth. Head down, he glanced around for any other Jews who might insult or jostle him. He'd chosen this life of distance from his people. The promise of success and wealth had enticed him to collect taxes for the Romans, but he'd sacrificed community with his people and his God. In fact he was worse off than a Gentile in his gilded life of isolation.

A ruckus began just down the street from his booth. The teacher everyone was talking about was passing by. Curious, he strained to catch a glimpse—and met the gaze of Jesus. Matthew had read the scriptures and heard the whispering of miracles happening in Capernaum. He was beginning to think that prophecies were coming into being right before his eyes. This man looked soul-deep. Although Matthew was one of the most despised in Israel, Jesus didn't look away. Instead He said, "Follow Me."

Later Jesus would further heal the broken places in Matthew's heart with His words: "You are My friends"

(John 15:14). Do you hold yourself apart from people or from God? Do you believe that your mistakes make relationships impossible? God is not distant, aloof, or angry. He invites you into friendship, just as He did Matthew. Follow Him and find a friend who will love you unconditionally.

- Are there things, attitudes, or habits in your life that you should leave behind to follow Jesus?

- In what ways does the knowledge that Jesus chose Matthew, a traitorous tax collector and outcast in society, as His disciple encourage you?

> *Lord, You want to be my friend in spite of all my mistakes! Help me to leave behind my sin.*

BANNER

In that day there shall be a Root of Jesse, who shall stand as a banner for the people. The Gentiles shall seek Him, and His rest shall be glorious.

ISAIAH 11:10

We were hopelessly lost. The blazing fall sun mocked us from overhead as we trudged in circles. My arms ached as I carried our exhausted two-year-old. Each time our hope of escape stirred, we'd round a corner and realize we'd been here before. Our other two girls sat down and cried from thirst and frustration—I wanted to join them and concede agonizing defeat to the corn maze. But then our daughter cried, "Look up!" There, over the cornstalks, we could see a flag fluttering. Finally we had a direction! Abandoning the confusing path, we blazed a trail through the scratchy stalks straight toward the flag. Like battle-weary soldiers we plodded out of the corn and into the open field.

Throughout history, banners were critical to victory in battle. During the chaos and clamor of war, banners signified not only your identity but also your position. They provided the critical rallying point and gave direction and unity to an otherwise fractured and frightened army.

Sometimes we too feel lost in the midst of our battle—

whether we're fighting cancer, friction at home, or bills we can't pay. When you're frustrated and feeling defeated, look to your banner to regain your purpose and direction. Hebrews tells us to fix our eyes on Jesus (Hebrews 12:2). God has not abandoned you. Look up! He is fighting for you. Under Christ's banner, we're united in His victory.

- According to Isaiah 11:10, who is the banner we must daily look to, rally around, and rest in?

- Whose strength are we intended to rely on at every moment according to Ephesians 6:10?

Lord, help me to keep my eyes fixed on You in the fog of life's battles.

GRACIOUS

You, O Lord, are a God full of compassion, and gracious, long-suffering, and abundant in mercy and truth.

Psalm 86:15

Not to those people. No, absolutely not.

Jonah, prophet of God, turned and sailed away. His hard heart eventually left him sitting on rock bottom. But God wasn't finished with him. He gave Jonah grace instead of the justice he deserved and pulled him out of the depths. Jonah reluctantly preached to the people of Nineveh, who repented. But Jonah wasn't happy about their turnaround. "I fled before to Tarshish, for I knew that You are a gracious God, and merciful, slow to anger, and of great kindness" (Jonah 4:2). Jonah was glad enough to receive God's grace, but when God extended it to the Ninevites, he was filled with rage.

Have you ever cringed over something God has asked you to do? Apart from God this world is without moral compass, spiritually unaware. But Jonah showed no love toward the Ninevites, no concern for their lives. Sometimes we're a bit too much like him. Jonah is a hard mirror to look into because his hypocrisy taunts us with our own. He wanted grace for himself but only punishment for others.

Ask God to show you the hard spots in your heart. Do

you forgive easily or hold on to offenses? Are you harboring a hard heart toward someone who's hurt you? Or maybe you have a general indifference toward telling others about God. Remember, God loves them as much as He loves you.

- Does some aspect of Jonah's hard heart exist in your attitude toward others?

- In what ways does recognizing your own unworthiness of God's grace help you extend mercy to others?

Lord, fill me with Your compassion, grace, and kindness toward the people You created and love.

COMFORTER

Blessed be God. . .the Father of mercies and the God of all comfort, who comforts us in all our tribulation, that we may be able to comfort those who are in any trouble, by the comfort with which we ourselves are comforted by God.

2 Corinthians 1:3–4

Two lines on the stick. I grinned and texted my husband. Guess what?! A third child, just as we'd been hoping. But our hopes were about to be dashed on the cruel rocks of a never-should-have-been moment. At our first ultrasound no lub-dub of a little heartbeat blipped on the screen. A week later, on my thirty-fourth birthday, I miscarried.

Maybe you've had days when nightmares that weren't supposed to invade your waking hours came to life in horrifying detail. Job had such a day where he "tore his robe and shaved his head and fell down on the ground"—I get this part of his reaction, but next he did something out of the ordinary—"and worshipped" (Job 1:20). He didn't scream his anger at God or crumble in hopelessness.

He worshipped.

Jesus said, "Blessed are those who mourn, for they shall be comforted" (Matthew 5:4). Nothing is wasted with God. In Him we are not abandoned, crushed in despair, or destroyed by our mourning. He promises to wrap His arms around us and show us purpose in our pain—He can transform the flow of our tears into a river of comfort for someone who's suffering.

- How has God comforted you by confirming His presence in your life?

- What relationships do you have that God might be using to bring you comfort and refreshment? How can you likewise use your experiences to comfort others?

Father God, You are here for me in every moment. Hold me when I'm hurting and fill my mind with Your peace. Open my eyes to the hurting people around me.

LIGHT

This then is the message that we have heard from Him and declare to you, that God is light and in Him is no darkness at all.

1 John 1:5

For four hundred years the Jewish people had heard silence from God. No prophet to enlighten them. No one to speak further of God's plans. So they waited, suffered. . .and hoped. But the roar of stillness met their ears.

Simeon was an old man, just and devout. The Holy Spirit had promised that he would see the Lord's Christ before he died. When he saw a young couple approaching the temple, he knew that this was the baby for whom the world had held its breath. Eyes gleaming, Simeon exclaimed, "My eyes have seen Your salvation that You have prepared before the face of all peoples, a light to lighten the Gentiles, and the glory of Your people Israel" (Luke 2:30–32).

Simeon anticipated the arrival of the Messiah. He remained faithful in a world that had largely lost hope after centuries of silence. Like Simeon we must live in anticipation of His return. We too must remain faithful in a world that is growing dark. "In Him was life, and the life was the light of men. And the light shines in darkness" (John 1:4–5). Jesus said that His followers would be the light of the world, to shine our hope for a future with Him for all the world to see.

- According to Ephesians 5:8–21, what does walking in the light look like? In what ways have you turned from light and walked in darkness instead?

- In times of great darkness, what does it mean in your life that Jesus is the Light of the World?

Lord, You are light! Make me a bright beacon to the world of everything that is good and right and true.

REFUGE

God is our refuge and strength, a very present help in trouble. Therefore we will not fear.

PSALM 46:1–2

As I write this, we're clenched in the icy fist of winter. We're experiencing a polar vortex with windchills reaching fifteen degrees below zero at night. We've had to plug in heaters for the chickens and the water troughs, feed extra hay, and close the horses in the barn. We layer on our Carhartts and wool socks, but the cold still slaps our cheeks scarlet three steps from the door. But once we head back into the house, a blanket of warm air envelops us in a cozy hug. The tension of shivering muscles begins to ooze from our bodies, and stinging fingers and toes slowly cease their throbbing. A steaming cup of coffee completes the warm-up process, driving the final chill from our bones.

Choosing to trust God feels a lot like coming in out of the cold. You no longer have to do life alone. You have help and a place of rest and comfort. Jesus invites you to come out of the cold world and into a loving relationship with Him: "He who dwells in the secret place of the Most High shall abide under the shadow of the Almighty" (Psalm 91:1).

Choose His refuge and live in His shelter. Release your

burdened mind to Him. He will tuck you under His wings and be a refuge for you in your hurt, frustration, fear, or failures. Abide with Him.

- What troubles or emotions are weighing you down and sapping your strength? Are you abiding with God or distracted by the things of this world?

- What will you do differently in the face of your problems if you are trusting in God?

God, You are a refuge for me because I choose You! I choose to trust You and obey You.

FREE

Having been made free from sin, then,
you became the servants of righteousness.
ROMANS 6:18

I'd failed miserably. The two-year-old under my teenage care had locked herself in the bathroom. I was beside myself with worry and shame. I heard giggles and the *flop flop* of the toilet paper roll. I could just imagine her twirling like a ribbon dancer with Charmin unfurling around her. Luckily her grandparents lived a few houses down. Her grandfather plucked the key from above the doorframe and unlocked the door. With a twinkle in his eye, he raised one brow at the older kids and headed back home. I'd been duped. They'd not only locked her in themselves but known exactly where to find the key.

From the time of Adam's first flub, we've all been born under the rule of sin. But as believers in Jesus we have been set free from sin. What a confusing thought since we also know that we still struggle with the addictive quality of sin even as we walk with Jesus. As Paul said, we do the things we don't want to do. It's as if we're locked in a prison with no tools to free ourselves. We desperately need someone to produce the key and open the door. Jesus is the only one who can free us because sin has no power over Him—He's free. And not only did He free us from sin, He handed us the keys through His Holy Spirit. Sin won't bring you happiness or satisfaction. Give it up for Jesus, and you'll be free.

- In what ways do you feel the tension of being freed from sin yet still struggling with it?

- In what ways has God's grace moved you into living a more disciplined life of holiness?

Lord, You set me free from sin's power. Give me the wisdom and strength through Your Holy Spirit to resist sin in my life.

TRINITY

The grace of the Lord Jesus Christ and the love of God and the communion of the Holy Spirit be with you all. Amen.

2 CORINTHIANS 13:14

Something just doesn't add up. God has sides that are a total mystery to us. Our minds strain to contain them, but the edge of an idea frays at the periphery of our mind and slips through our grasp. With God 1 + 1 + 1 = 1. Our words stagger under the weight of the Trinity. God is our Father in heaven. God is the Son who walked this earth and created it. God is the Holy Spirit who indwells His believers. And yet they are one: "The LORD our God is one LORD" (Deuteronomy 6:4).

But don't stumble over these secrets. You don't need to fully understand God's edges and corners to trust Him and know Him. He is a mystery to us, but not completely. He tells His story in scripture. Through His interactions with us, we can know His character, His will, His great love for us, and His plan to redeem us through Jesus.

Hebrews tells us that "faith is the substance of things hoped for, the evidence of things not seen" (Hebrews 11:1). With God, believing is seeing. Faith opens our spiritual eyes to a kingdom that is not of this world. When Nicodemus sought out Jesus in the middle of the night with questions,

Jesus told him, "Unless a man is born again, he cannot see the kingdom of God" (John 3:3). Praise God that we have a God more magnificent than we can understand, yet who loves us beyond compare.

- What benefits do you see in God being triune?
- Read Ephesians 1:2–14 and consider how the Trinity works together to accomplish salvation.

God, even though I don't fully grasp Your triune nature, I'm forever grateful that You saved my soul.

LISTENING

I love the LORD *because He has heard my voice and my supplications. Because He has inclined His ear to me, therefore I will call on Him as long as I live.*

PSALM 116:1–2

"I found ten housecleaning services near here." She bolted to her feet, heart hammering, as coffee sloshed onto her paperwork. Alexa's soothing AI voice had nearly given her a heart attack by answering her spoken wish for help. That would teach her to talk to herself in an empty house. Alexa was always listening.

Alexa's listening ear may prove unhelpful, but someone much more powerful and caring than Alexa also has His ear turned toward you. God is always listening for your voice. The Bible says that He hears, He's near, and He has inclined His ear toward you. "Before they call, I will answer, and while they are still speaking, I will hear" (Isaiah 65:24). Although His answers may not always be in the way we expect or want, have no doubt that He always answers. The problem is not that God is hard of hearing but often that we largely ignore Him in our day to day.

Jesus' disciples got a crash course in prayer. He told them to skip the flowery words and simply praise God and ask

Him for their needs. Paul told the believers that their prayer
should be like breathing—that they should "pray withou
ceasing" (1 Thessalonians 5:17). We have the wondrous privilege of talking with the all-powerful God of all creation. H
listens because He loves us! So first, pray. Then pray, and pray
again!

- Read Matthew 6:5–15. Does this alter any of your preconceptions about prayer or show you prayer habits you need to change?

- In what ways could you make prayer a continual part of your day?

Father God, help me to live in the ongoing posture of prayer.

DELIVERER

You are my hiding place. You shall preserve me from trouble.
You shall surround me with songs of deliverance.
Psalm 32:7

She was drowning. Pulled under by torment, Mary Magdalene could no longer see the point of living. Her life was not her own. Her lucid moments horrified her. And the other times. . .she'd rather not know the true depths of her possession. Seven demons drove her. Seven—the number of completion. Her life was completely out of control.

But then she met someone, and everything changed. She changed. She was no longer what she had been. Now she was something totally different. She was free. She was forgiven. She was. . .delivered. Jesus looked into her shame and said, "You are Mine." And He threw the demons out of her life. For the first time in ages, she felt peace.

Beloved, what bondage is holding your head under the turbulent flood of this life—the hollowness of grief, the battle of addiction, the exhaustion of depression, breath-stealing anxiety, sickness, financial hardship, broken relationships, abuse? Jesus sees the crushing struggle of your life. He doesn't promise that it will be easy, but He does promise to help you through it. When your life is in chaos, surrender to His control. "I sought the Lord, and He heard me and delivered me from all my fears" (Psalm 34:4). He can deliver you into calm too.

- In what areas of your life do you need deliverance?
- God's deliverance does not always mean that He removes hard things from our lives. How else might God deliver you, and what is Jesus' part in that deliverance?

Lord, deliver me from evil. Whether the sea of my life is clear as glass or choppy and turbulent waters, I have peace because You have overcome the world.

INCOMPREHENSIBLE

Great is the L*ORD, and greatly to be praised,*
and His greatness is unsearchable.
Psalm 145:3

Her small blond head bounced off the glass door. Maybe washing the fingerprints off the windows hadn't been a good idea. . .if for no other reason than the personal safety of my energetic five-year-old. As I put her warm ice pack back in the freezer, she called, "Thank you! Tell me when two minutes are up." I shook my head and laughed. "Honey, this won't be frozen in two minutes." She shrugged and skipped away. "Okay, three minutes then."

In one sense our grasp on God doesn't exceed a child's comprehension of time. The apostle Paul raved about our inability to etch the cavernous expanse of His being on our minds: "O the depth of the riches both of the wisdom and knowledge of God! How unsearchable are His judgments and His ways past finding out!" (Romans 11:33). His way of doing things at times confounds us. And in His wisdom God doesn't always answer all the questions His children ask. He is in a category of His own, unclassified with any other.

But God didn't create us only to leave our mouths gaping in wonder yet our hearts in despair over a distant supreme being we can never know. In His impressive wisdom He sent us Jesus—God with us. So if you want to know God better, look at Jesus. May our goal be like Paul's: to "know Him and the power of His resurrection" (Philippians 3:10). Pour God's Word over your life until you are saturated by it. Search out His ways for every situation.

- In what ways have you come to know our incomprehensible God, and how does this grow your faith?
- Have you ever tried to reduce God to manageable terms for your own benefit?

Lord, Your ways are so far above mine,
and yet I can know You. Show me more!

GLORY

"I am the Lord*—that is My name—and I will not give My glory to another or My praise to carved images."*

Isaiah 42:8

"No way! Dad! Is this you?" My husband had turned up an old picture of his high school soccer team, faces smeared with paint and wearing serious expressions. He laughed and challenged our daughters to pick him out of the group. Most of us have at least one scrapbook, box of ribbons, or trophy from childhood wins as a memorial to the glory of our youth.

God also told the Israelites to set up memorials. But not because He needed shrines to Himself. God is never in need of reminders. The memorials were for His people—so they would never forget His glory. He instructed them, "Beware, lest you forget the Lord who brought you out of the land of Egypt, from the house of bondage" (Deuteronomy 6:12).

We tend to be a forgetful group. The Israelites certainly forgot how God had freed them. But what if *we* remembered better where we were before and the mess God pulled us from? The Israelites got busy living their lives, and they forgot God's glory, His provision when they needed it, and His healing. So do we. And just like they did, each time we find ourselves facing an impossible dilemma, we need those remembrances of who He is—the most powerful, valuable, significant being. He is glorious!

- In light of 1 Corinthians 10:31, what does it look like to glorify God in our lives, and how can we live this practically?

- Since we tend to forget what God has done for us just as the Israelites did, how can you intentionally remember God and His work in your life on a regular basis?

God, You have done great things for us. Your glory is unmatched.

RELATIONAL

Because you are sons, God has sent forth the Spirit of His Son into your hearts, crying, "Abba, Father!"
GALATIANS 4:6

"Fine."

"Good."

"Okay."

My oldest daughter is the queen of the one-word answer. Even when things clearly aren't hunky-dory in her world, her initial response is "Fine." She would prefer to hide; but because I love her awkward, independent, preteen self so fiercely, I can't leave our relationship to flounder at *fine*. It's hard to watch her pick up the pattern that I, and most likely you too, have learned—stuffing our struggles. Too often we choose isolation over relationship because we've been burned before. But we were made to be relational creatures, because God is relational. And we are His image bearers.

God has always lived in relationship because He has always been a trinity. He created us not out of boredom but love, and He wants a relationship with you. You can open up to His love for you without fear. You can show Him your scars. He's already seen them anyway. And Jesus can show you His. He wants you to discover the true depths of His love for you through His nail-scarred hands. Beloved, He wants to love you in a big way. He wants to be part of your life. Open the door to close, authentic relationship with God, and His overflowing love can transform your relationships with the people around you.

- What implications does God's deep, relational love for us have for the way we interact with others (Mark 12:30–31)?

- In what ways have you recently tried to deepen your relationship with God and with others? If you haven't, what new habits could you form?

Father God, I'm awed that You want a relationship with me. Show me more of Your love and how I can pour it out on those around me.

IN CONTROL

"Your kingdom come. Your will be done on earth as it is in heaven."

MATTHEW 6:10

Gobsmacked, my college friend and I looked from our dressed-up dates to each other and lost it in peals of laughter. We'd bet our fun-loving, practical-joking boyfriends that they couldn't have a serious, sophisticated evening of conversation with us. They'd arrived in their finest, escorted us to the car, opened our doors. . .and proceeded to speak in British accents for the duration of the evening. They promised us a scrummy dinner and were quite chuffed about their posh manners. As they waffled on about tea and crumpets, we realized that, as expected, they'd over-egged the pudding. We could have been miffed, but instead we married our cheeky rascals and have spent close to two decades relaxing in the comic relief they bring to our lives, even when it's far from what we had in mind. Oh, and we totally won that wager.

God's plans will come to pass. His will is unavoidable, inevitable, and sure. He is the supreme sovereign of this spinning sphere. We waste a lot of our time and energy scurrying around trying to force all the pieces into the places we think they should go. Just as I came to appreciate my husband's less serious take on life, we can relax in God's plans. They're good ones, friend—plans "of peace and not of evil" (Jeremiah 29:11).

Sometimes we don't see His side of it clearly when hard times hit, but the power of global event planning that spans the ages rests at His fingertips. Trust in His goodness, faithfulness, and power.

- In what areas of your life do you need to release your tightfisted grip on control and yield to God's will?

- What comfort can we find in uncertain times from knowing that God's will always comes to pass?

Lord, give me peace in trusting You to run things.

TIRELESS

Have you not known? Have you not heard that the everlasting God, the Lord, the Creator of the ends of the earth, does not lose strength, nor is weary? There is no searching of His understanding. He gives power to the faint, and He increases the strength of those who have no might.

Isaiah 40:28–29

Rising tensions splash onto the global stage daily—political unrest, financial uncertainty, armed conflicts. And closer to home, rising expectations at work or school leave us feeling overcommitted, exhausted, and downright cranky. Each twenty-four-hour span buzzes with a week's worth of activity. Whether you thrive on the constant connection of many commitments or feel pressed by an unavoidable workload, many of us are yearning for a slowdown.

God's prophet Elijah knew too well the headaches, heartaches, and body aches of keeping hectic, heavy hours. He was emotionally, physically, and spiritually spent from his clash with the prophets of Baal on Mount Carmel. But instead of rest he received a death threat from Queen Jezebel. He literally ran himself into the ground when he collapsed from exhaustion and told God he wanted to die (1 Kings 19:4). But God didn't ridicule him. In His compassion God saw that, like a hangry toddler, Elijah needed rest, food, and encouragement. And He provided.

Our God is still tireless today. He "does not lose strength, nor is weary" (Isaiah 40:28). Draw from His bottomless well of strength. We wear out, but our God never will.

- Meditate on Isaiah 40. Why should we not give up when we're on the verge of exhaustion and despair?

- Look again at verses 27–31 and consider what can help you persevere through discouragement and tiredness.

God, I'm so glad that You don't tire or grow weary—because I sure do. I need Your Word, and Your presence, to strengthen me.

HELPER

"The Comforter, who is the Holy Spirit, whom the Father will send in My name, He shall teach you all things."

John 14:26

"That's the one!" My breath twirled in ribbons of frozen vapor. *Excellent, my job is complete*, I thought. The weather was subzero and not my ideal for picking out a Christmas tree, so I jumped back into the car and molded myself into the heated seat while my husband loaded the tree. I knew I wasn't being overly helpful, so when he slid behind the wheel half-frozen, I smiled sweetly and winked. "We make a great team."

"We?" His eyebrows climbed to his hairline. "Do I have a mouse in my pocket?"

As believers we do, in fact, have a helper in our pocket. And the Holy Spirit is infinitely more help than a tiny rodent—or me. God's Spirit lives in us, to aid and empower us. How incredible is this news for the followers of Jesus! The Spirit of the miracle-making, covenant-keeping God of everything that ever was, is, and is to come lives in us. It's unfathomable, and yet it's true. Jesus promised His disciples that He would send them help—the Holy Spirit. "I will pray to the Father, and He shall give you another Comforter, that He may abide with you forever" (John 14:16).

Listen for The Holy Spirit's direction. Sometimes we're sitting in the car and He says, "Be still," while He works things out. Other times He wants us to get out in the cold and do something. Either way, God does the heavy lifting as we stand in awe of His unfolding plans.

- Consider John 16:4–15. In what ways is the Holy Spirit our helper?

- What things prevent you from seeing God as your ultimate helper?

Lord, I thank You for the gift of Your Spirit. Help me to hear Your voice and to keep in step with the Spirit.

MIGHTY

"You reign over all. And in Your hand is power and might, and in Your hand it is to make great and to give strength to all."
1 CHRONICLES 29:12

Superwoman: an exceptional woman who desires to be exemplary in all endeavors. Is this your life's creed? It was mine. Modern culture has convinced us that we can, and should, do it all—perfectly—with a bright smile and a stylish wardrobe. But the Superwoman identity leads only to anxiety, guilt, and burnout. Shouldn't a proper Proverbs 31 woman also have superpowers?

The Mighty Mom perception was beginning to ring false. I felt like a failure on all fronts, weak and inadequate. But how fabulous for me that those are God's favorite kinds of people. I was just forgetting to lean on Him. You see, Superwoman and God's woman are not synonymous. Superwoman doesn't usually have time for God, and she thinks saving the day is in her job description. But the Proverbs 31 woman "opens her mouth with wisdom" (verse 26) because her life is saturated with scripture and she draws strength from God.

Stop listening to the voices that preach, "Girl, you've got this," and instead remember that *God's* got this. He is mighty.

He is fully capable. You can lean on Him when your strength is gone. You can turn to Him when you need a shoulder to cry on. You can grab His hand when you need reassurance. You can ask Him when you need advice. He's got you covered.

- How have you felt in the past about your role as a woman when you read Proverbs 31, empowered or discouraged?
- In what ways does knowing that the Proverbs 31 woman draws her strength and stability from God change your perceptions?

Father, I've been trying to do things without You. Please help me to lean on You.

UNDERSTANDING

O Lord, You have searched me and known me.
You know when I sit down and when I rise up;
You understand my thought from afar.

Psalm 139:1–2

"Check the garage." That's my dad's happy place. Cars, trucks, tractors, boats—he loves all things mechanical and can recall the engine in every truck and tractor he ever owned. He understands what makes them tick and how to fix them when they stop. So naturally every time my car sputters, his is the first number I dial.

In Psalm 139 David wrote that God, who created and designed every facet of your being and planned out the days of your life, knows you. He understands you completely because He designed you. He knows exactly what you need when nothing in your life seems to be working right because "His understanding is infinite" (Psalm 147:5).

The book of Hebrews goes on to confirm that Jesus too understands us intimately. "For we do not have a high priest who cannot be concerned with the feeling of our weaknesses, but was in all points tempted as we are, yet without sin. Therefore let us come boldly to the throne of grace, that we may obtain mercy and find grace to help in time of need" (Hebrews 4:15–16).

Friend, Jesus understands every struggle you've been through. He welcomes you to come to Him for the help you need.

- Read Psalm 139:1 and Hebrews 4:12–13. How well does God know you and understand your life?
- In what ways does knowing the depth of God's understanding of us offer you hope and encouragement in seeking His help?

Lord, You know all of my feelings, thoughts, and motivations. You see into the core of me and understand my struggles. Help me turn to You when I need help.

WONDERFUL

Perfect love casts out fear.

1 John 4:18

"Flat stones work the best." One sunny morning I taught my daughters how to flick their wrists just so, sending rocks hopping across the pond's surface like startled frogs. While this entertainment is harmless, sometimes we heft a different kind of stone and take aim. And while these rocks aren't made of granite or quartz, the impact of judgment, condemnation, and shame can be just as painful. Social media lets us showcase the less-than-wonderful aspects of our character freely and often anonymously. We present a Facebook-perfect front so we're less vulnerable—because we expect the world to throw sticks and stones.

But Jesus never did. The Pharisees dragged a sinful woman in front of Jesus. Though we might sin differently than she did, we can identify with her shame. She must have been so shaken. So afraid. Her vulnerability, her mistakes, laid bare. Her accusers didn't recognize her for the daughter of God that she was. They didn't even see her at all. But they demanded her death. And they demanded it from the only perfect one who could condemn her.

But Jesus didn't throw any rocks. Instead He did something unexpected. Something astonishing. Jesus is surprisingly wonderful in all that He is. He's refreshingly gentle and kind where we are too often harsh and rude. His grace was the perfect foil to their anger and spite. "Has no man condemned you?" He asked. "Neither do I condemn you. Go and sin no more" (John 8:10–11). Oh, His unsurpassed love for us even in our mess. Surprising. Amazing. Wonderful.

- In what ways do you condemn others without seeing them as loved by God?
- How could you behave in surprisingly wonderful ways, like Jesus, in the midst of others' sinful behavior, rudeness, or mistreatment?

Lord, Your grace is so astonishingly wonderful.
Help me to imitate Your ways.

VICTORY

"Death is swallowed up in victory. O death,
where is your sting? O grave, where is your victory?"
1 CORINTHIANS 15:54–55

Blood dripped from the hyssop. Moses brushed it across the lintel and touched it to the doorposts on either side. The first Passover was approaching, when the blood of sacrifice would deliver God's people from death as He drove Egypt to her knees. God snapped the chains of their slavery and led them into His promised land—victory!

The exodus was a powerful picture of God's deliverance, but it was a mere shadow of the victory He had planned for a Passover many years later. Jesus ate with His disciples, knowing that the blood of the final Passover lamb was about to be spilled—and that on the third day He would rise again and break the stronghold of death. "O death, where is your sting? O grave, where is your victory?" (1 Corinthians 15:55). He freed us from a bondage far crueler than anything the Egyptians had laid on His people. He freed us from the power of sin and death. He brought us back from death and moved us into life everlasting.

Now we can fix our eyes on the hope of a land more wonderful than Canaan, "a better country—that is, a heavenly one" (Hebrews 11:16), because He transferred our citizenship to heaven (Philippians 3:20). His victory is ours. "For whatever is born of God overcomes the world, and this is the victory that overcomes the world, even our faith" (1 John 5:4).

Death has been swallowed up in victory!

- When did the truth of the gospel become personal to you?

- What are some benefits of knowing that Jesus has overcome the world?

Heavenly Father, "thanks be to [You], who gives us the victory through our Lord Jesus Christ" (1 Corinthians 15:57).

INVISIBLE

No man has seen God at any time. If we love one another, God dwells in us and His love is perfected in us.

1 John 4:12

The windows rattled like chattering teeth, and the power blinked out. The house seemed to brace for the wind's devastating fist. We grabbed the kids and blankets and scurried to take shelter in our basement for the rest of the night. The next day we gaped at the aftermath of the storm as we ventured a few miles to help a neighbor. Trees, fence rails, and power lines littered the roads. Forests were leveled. Ancient trees, the earth ripped from their grasp, lay like rows of casualties. Their roots reached skeletal fingers toward pockmarked houses. The intense, straight-line derecho winds had ransacked the landscape like a frenzied looter.

Our God may not be visible to us, but His power and sovereignty are as undeniable as the force of the wind. The Israelites struggled to leave behind their tangible idols from Egypt and follow an invisible God, even after He'd proven Himself miraculously capable. God didn't give them, or us, any images of Himself; He did something better. He gave us Jesus to show us His character and love for us, and He gave us an entire universe filled with His wonders, including us—His creations made in His image.

His power can reshape the landscape of your life if you'll trust Him.

- What comfort do you gain from the evidence that God is in control of this world even though you can't see Him?

- What evidence of His work have you seen in your own life and in the lives of others?

God, You are no less real and far more powerful than the wind. Teach me to trust Your plans.

KIND

That in the ages to come He might show the exceeding riches of His grace in His kindness toward us through Christ Jesus.

Ephesians 2:7

"I'm going to say something, Lord." There! She'd decided. She wouldn't enjoy the conversation, but having made up her mind, she felt lighter. Her husband's health had declined, and he couldn't do the things he used to. He really needed some help. Her son was busy, and he and his father shared a rocky relationship, but enough was enough. She was going to ask for his help. Later her grandson burst through the door. "What are you doing today?" she asked. "Oh, Dad and I are helping Grandpa work on his truck." She almost dropped the spoon in her hand. She hadn't said a word to her son yet. God had taken care of her husband's needs and her son's heart without her input at all.

God sent another woman just what she needed during a famine. This Gentile woman from Zarephath was preparing to cook her last meal when Elijah showed up. She decided to trust God and never ran out of flour or oil. We, like her, are not out here floundering by ourselves. We have a kind and loving heavenly Father who notices every detail of our pain and needs—and also the places in our hearts that need to soften toward one another. He would never have gone to such great lengths if He didn't love us. His greatest act of kindness was Jesus.

Pray about your needs. God is not harsh, but gracious, kind, and generous.

- In what ways does knowing that we deserve God's wrath but have received His kindness increase your desire to love and serve Him?

- According to Romans 2:4, what is the goal of God's kindness?

God, You have shown us unimaginable kindness through Jesus. Help me to be as kind and gentle with those around me.

JUST

Righteousness and judgment are the habitation of His throne.
Psalm 97:2

"Guilty." The gavel rings with finality. We have a sin problem. The Bible says that "the wages of sin is death" (Romans 6:23) and "all have sinned and come short of the glory of God" (Romans 3:23). That is a huge, horrifying death sentence for all humanity, because we know that God is absolutely and perfectly just. That is our deserved sentence because we've all ignored God, gone our own way, and done whatever we wanted.

But praise be to our merciful God who is both fully gracious and fully just. And praise Him even more that neither of those verses in Romans are punctuated with Him sentencing us to die with no exemptions. "But"—Romans 6:23 continues with some of the most beautiful words in scripture—"the gift of God is eternal life through Jesus Christ our Lord."

What relief the wonder of Christ's atonement brings to our souls. Jesus, who is fully God, died in agony on the cross to change our sin situation. Paul declared, "We conclude that a man is justified by faith" (Romans 3:28). All that is required of us unworthy sinners is to confess our transgressions: "If we confess our sins, He is faithful and just to forgive us our sins and to cleanse us from all unrighteousness" (1 John 1:9). His suffering sent us saving grace. We are justified and now serving life with Christ.

- Consider Romans 3:23–26. How can God be just and still spare the sinner?

- Read Psalm 32. How does a sinner move from a sentence of "death" to "life"?

Lord God, You give us grace!
I am ecstatically, eternally grateful
that You died to save me from my sins.

HUMOROUS

A merry heart does good like a medicine,
but a broken spirit dries the bones.
PROVERBS 17:22

I was mad. Honestly, the reason escapes me now, but my husband assures me that he was the undeserving target of my ire. He's probably right. But while I was dressing him down, secretly he was dressing me up. He snuck behind me and draped a kitchen towel across my shoulders like a cape. "There!" he announced with a flourish. "Now you're super angry!" Silence screamed through the kitchen. The ice maker dumped. The kids snickered. My husband grinned. Then I giggled too. The tension popped like bubbles on the breeze.

Have you ever wondered if God finds things in life as funny as we do? The Bible says there is "a time to laugh" (Ecclesiastes 3:4). We are created in God's image, and we definitely understand and express humor. We can also learn from humor, even if it's in hindsight. Imagine Jonah, years later, trading fish stories with his friends. "You'll never believe the one that got away from me!"

Comedy is captivating. We enjoy being around people who make us laugh, and it softens our hard moments. Captivate your audience with the humor of God. Draw them to a heavenly Father who can laugh with us. If we relieve the tension of a few of our failures, often others are more willing to let their guard down and listen to the gospel.

- Have you ever learned life lessons from a funny situation?
- In what ways has laughter softened some of the hard edges of a difficult circumstance and allowed you to grow?

God, thank You for the release of laughter.
Show me the appropriate places to laugh with
others and soften the strife we sometimes encounter.

FRIEND

"I do not call you servants, for the servant does not know what his master does, but I have called you friends."

JOHN 15:15

Have you ever met someone who just seemed to click with you right from the start? You think, *I really like her. She totally gets me!* Over time you can talk about life in the shorthand of friends, and even years of separation don't seem to matter. You pick up a conversation whenever you're together as if no time has passed. But maybe instead of a soul sister, you've experienced shallow friends who abandoned or betrayed you when it would have cost them something to be faithful to you.

Scripture tells us that there is a friend who sticks closer than a brother (Proverbs 18:24). Who is this friend? It's Jesus. If your experience with friends has been a bad one, don't worry that He'll mistreat you, because Jesus has already given you everything. He gave His life for yours. "No man has greater love than this, that a man lay down his life for his friends" (John 15:13). Beloved, He has called you His friend. And He will never leave you or forsake you (Deuteronomy 31:8).

Jesus didn't mean for us to come to Him for one brief moment and then move on with our lives, nodding to Him on Sunday as if He were an acquaintance in the grocery aisle. He wants to be your closest confidant. In every second—in your work, in your rest, in your fun, even in your pain—tarry with Him in friendship.

- What does it mean to you to have a personal friend who is inconceivably vast in every aspect?

- Read Psalm 71 and consider verse 6. In what ways have you leaned on God throughout your life?

> *God, it is unimaginably wondrous that*
> *You want a close friendship with me.*
> *Help me to be a truer friend to others.*

WRATHFUL

Having now been justified by His blood,
we shall be saved from wrath through Him.
Romans 5:9

Dead. He couldn't believe it. It was the most confounding thing. Some friends of ours run a dairy farm, and once on a late-night cow check, the husband came across a heifer lying next to their swinging cow brush. These contraptions look like giant hanging bottle brushes for the cows to rub on and groom themselves. After some investigation he discovered that theirs had shorted out and electrocuted the unsuspecting cow.

The rooster had barely crowed the dawn of time when God's first couple had their initial brush with sin. Eve and Adam fell for Satan's lies, and the shock of sin jolted them from life into spiritual death and eventually their physical death. God is holy and without sin. Like water thrown on a grease fire, He rejects sin. Because God's wrath is aimed at our sin, He gave us a way back into life: "He who believes in the Son has everlasting life, and he who does not believe the Son shall not see life, but the wrath of God remains on him" (John 3:36).

Jesus came to be the propitiation—the atoning sacrifice—for sin: "For as through one man's disobedience many were made sinners, so through the obedience of One many shall be made righteous" (Romans 5:19). God loves us so much that He vented His wrath toward sin on Jesus at the cross. Jesus chose to take the consequence for our sins on Himself so we could be righteous for all eternity.

- When you read about God's wrath, what comes to mind? Can God be both wrath and love at the same time?

- Consider Luke 19:41–44 and what it reveals about both God's love and His judgment.

Heavenly Father, I'm eternally grateful that Jesus died so that I am no longer an object of Your wrath.

GOD WHO SEES ME

She called the name of the LORD who spoke to her "You, God, See Me."
GENESIS 16:13

The cold plastic chair moaned as she shifted in search of a more comfortable position, as if that would ease the turmoil of her mind. No one noticed her. They were too lost in their own lives to see that she was sixteen, alone, pregnant, and sitting in a women's clinic agonizing over her choices, both past and future.

Roll back a few centuries of time and you'll hear the soul-wrenching sobs of another lonely and misused pregnant woman. Hagar collapsed by a wilderness spring in her flight from Sarah's fury. She'd rubbed her pregnancy in Sarah's face, and her barb had buried itself deep in the bull's-eye of Sarah's pain—the ache of her childlessness. Sarah had lashed out harshly at her servant girl. But Hagar's difficult circumstances had not gone unnoticed. The Lord went to the wilderness to find her. The compassionate Father God had seen her pain, her affliction, and offered her hope and a future if she'd trust Him. Someone saw her. In her overwhelming relief and gratitude, Hagar cried, "You, God, see me."

Beloved of God, I don't know what you're suffering

today. But whether it's isolation, misunderstanding, abuse, addiction, disease. . .God sees you. He looks after you with tender care. And He has good plans for you—not that you would be crushed by your circumstances but created anew in Christ Jesus.

- Meditate on 2 Corinthians 4:8–18. What hope do these verses offer you in hard times?

- God loves you, sees you, and longs to bless you. Are there sins in your life that may be blocking His blessings or ways that you could trust Him more?

God, You are not a distant God who doesn't care. You see my pain and suffering. Help me to trust and follow You.

SHEPHERD

The LORD is my shepherd. I shall not want. . . .
Your rod and Your staff, they comfort me.
PSALM 23:1, 4

My middle daughter is nine years old. Her initials spell ELF, and she fills her size 1 boots with a powerful personality in a petite package. Her lack of fear is unfortunately sometimes her folly. She's frosted my locks with more than a few gray hairs because this small person shares my love of horses. Her mare is one thousand pounds with attitude. One day my heart stuttered when I caught her small self standing directly behind those massive hindquarters, blissfully blind to the fact that her tail braiding was irritating Miss Sassy.

We all need pulled out of harm's way at times, and sometimes out of our own way. Thankfully, we have a good shepherd—one who knows how to use His tools to maximum effect. Psalm 23 says that in the dark and dangerous places of life, we can rest easy knowing He carries a rod and a staff. A good shepherd is both gentle and bold in his fierce protection of his sheep. He hurtles his rod through the air to strike a death blow to a predator or even to get the attention of a headstrong sheep headed for trouble. He might also guide the sheep with gentle taps from his staff or slide its curved end around a lamb's neck to lift it out of danger. A good shepherd would die to protect his sheep. . .and they rest easy in his tender care.

- Why do you think God compares us to sheep? What similarities do you find?

- Does learning more about the ways that shepherds cared for their sheep give you comfort in your relationship with God?

Lord, You are the good shepherd. Thank You for guiding, correcting, and comforting me. Thank You for giving Your life to save mine.

PERFECT

As for God, His way is perfect.
Psalm 18:30

She'd blown it. She'd promised herself it was the last time, but she'd done it again. Does her shame sound familiar? I can't capture the crux of this very real struggle any better than the apostle Paul: "I do not do the good that I want, but I do the evil that I do not want" (Romans 7:19). In essence we all fall short of God's glory. That is. . .all except one.

Two thousand years ago Jesus walked into the wilderness to be tempted by the father of lies. Satan wanted to dirty Jesus' perfection and disqualify Him from savior status. He was counting on a repeat of Eden. But Jesus crushed Satan's hopes for victory with three words: "It is written. . ." The hope of humanity took wing as the great tempter failed and Jesus remained unstained by sin.

Jesus is the only perfect one who could free us from our slavery to sin. He traded places with us. "[God] has made Him who knew no sin to be sin for us, that we might be made the righteousness of God in Him" (2 Corinthians 5:21). Beloved, "by [His] wounds you were healed" (1 Peter 2:24). Forgiven. Paid in full. Redeemed. Jesus lived the perfect life He knew we never could. Now we're free to find the mercy and strength that we need in His grace (Hebrews 4:16).

You don't have to do it alone. You don't have to be perfect. Jesus did that for you.

- In what areas of your life do you feel the tension between your imperfection and your desire for the excellence of following Jesus?

- What can we learn from Jesus' response to Satan's temptations (Matthew 4:1–11)?

God, You are the only perfect one. Give me strength and the wisdom of scripture to resist the temptations that I face.

HOPE

Let us hold fast the profession of our faith without wavering, for He who promised is faithful.

HEBREWS 10:23

"When I get a unicorn toy for my birthday. . ." I had to adore her confidence. *When*, not *if*. My four-year-old held on to the hope of her birthday desires with the full expectation that they would be fulfilled.

What is this same attractive quality that draws unbelievers toward those who follow Jesus? How is it that hopeful confidence saturates our words with expectation and our actions with meaning? How do believers not end up down a rutted road of discouragement and bitterness? What is our reason to keep going? Because in the midst of lives that might not have turned out quite as we were expecting—the sting of failure, the ache of suffering, the fatigue of caring for an aging parent—there's God. And He is our hope. He is oh so faithful and the great keeper of His promises.

We have the sturdy hope that our homesickness for heaven will not last forever. Someday all this hurt, heartache, and hardship will be gone. We have been born again into "a living hope" through Jesus into "an inheritance incorruptible and undefiled, and which does not fade away, reserved in heaven for you" (1 Peter 1:3–4). God gives us hope of a future beyond this present world. Hope of an existence that transcends our mortal bodies. Hope of eternity with Him. Hope of a better, more Jesus-like, life now. And we too can be confident in our hope. *When*, not *if*.

- In hope-crushing circumstances have you ever placed your hope in the wrong things? Which ones, and what was the outcome?

- In what ways does your hope of heaven infuse your life now with meaning and joy?

Lord, our lives here may be broken, but You have not left us in pieces with no hope. Someday my hope of heaven will be reality.

LIVING WATER

"To him who is thirsty I will freely give of the fountain of the water of life. He who overcomes shall inherit all things, and I will be his God, and he shall be My son."

REVELATION 21:6–7

She struggled to swallow. The smooth coffee flavor with notes of chocolate and nuts that she'd been expecting had been substituted with what tasted like gas-station swill. Her morning java was no joke, and she'd been accused of being a coffee snob. But she knew exactly what had happened. Her economical husband had bought the cheap stuff. It left her grumpy, unsatisfied, and thirsting for something better.

There's a battle going on over what we will swallow in this world. We all have an appetite for something. Is it God? Or is it something else entirely? Jesus urges us to conquer our thirst for this world and satisfy our cravings with Him. God created us with certain needs and desires. We're all looking for that one taste that meets our every expectation. Jesus knows that seeking fulfillment in anything this world has to offer our palates will ultimately leave us yearning for the real deal. And He offers living water—a relationship, a way of life that will satisfy your longings and your soul's deepest needs. Through Him you can conquer everything that competes for your attention.

Come to Jesus. Drink of the living waters and never look back.

- What things in life are competing for your thirst?
- Do you view Christianity through the lens of what Christ asks you to give up or through the lens of everything you gain in Jesus?

Lord, "as the deer pants for the water brooks, so my soul pants for You. . . . My soul thirsts for God, for the living God. When shall I come and appear before God?" (Psalm 42:1–2).

CORNERSTONE

You are no longer strangers and foreigners but fellow citizens with the saints and of the household of God, and are built upon the foundation of the apostles and prophets, Jesus Christ Himself being the chief cornerstone.

EPHESIANS 2:19–20

A moment of panic gripped me. The top two layers of the three-tier wedding cake I'd just assembled for my cousin's reception lay splattered across the floor, and the guests would be arriving in half an hour. Flowers adorned the space between the raised layers, but the dowel rods I'd used were too thin to support such height. They listed perilously before their grasp on the top layer slipped and it plopped onto the floor—followed by a sideways slide of the second layer. Much to my relief, I was able to reconstruct the layers with thicker dowels before the guests arrived.

Foundations are vital. If we focus too much on the wrong aspects of life, we too will crumble under the pressure. Millennia ago, God told of the foundation stone He was going to provide: "Behold, I lay in Zion a stone for a foundation, a tested stone, a precious cornerstone, a sure foundation" (Isaiah 28:16). The cornerstone of a building was laid first. It was a tried stone carefully shaped to square the building and to provide a solid foundation able to bear the weight of the structure that was built on top of it.

Jesus is that precious cornerstone laid by God. Build your life on belief in Him and square your actions around the example of His life, and your foundation will not tremble in the quakes of this world.

- What areas of your life are not built with Jesus as the first priority and cornerstone?

- What in your life does not help you to be conformed to the image of Christ?

Lord, help me to build my life around the cornerstone of Jesus.

JUDGE

His work is perfect, for all His ways are judgment,
a God of truth and without iniquity; just and right is He.
DEUTERONOMY 32:4

"She hit me!" is echoed by "He took my Legos!" and quickly followed by "I'm telling Mom!" Parenting kids requires loads of discretion and mom discernment. Many days we're left longing for the wisdom of Solomon to sort out the tangled chaos of injured feelings, false accusations, and hidden agendas. Oh, for a polygraph machine! Whether it's kids or coworkers, family or friends, sometimes we can sleuth out the truth. At other times we're left in confusion about the real story.

We can tend toward judgment in all situations: *Was she actually trying to help me or make me feel inadequate? Am I doing this only because I feel guilty?* God does want us to distinguish between right and wrong, but not to confuse judgmentalism with right judgment. Jesus said, "Do not judge according to the appearance, but judge with righteous judgment" (John 7:24).

Sometimes we get it wrong, but unlike us God always judges rightly. Not only does He know everything and see everything, but He is the source of all wisdom. He gets things right every single time.

Ignoring sin isn't the way of love, but neither is harsh criticism. If we're out of line, we need someone to point out our error—in gentle, caring concern for our emotional, spiritual, and physical well-being—so we can correct our behavior. Good judgment is both gentle and loving.

- What should our attitude be in judging life's many situations?

- How should we balance confronting sin and the fact that God is the only perfect judge?

Heavenly Father, You alone are without sin and able to judge perfectly.

COUNSELOR

I will instruct you and teach you in the way that you shall go. I will guide you with My eye.
PSALM 32:8

He rolled to a stop six feet from the cliff's edge. When my husband was sixteen, he went hiking on a class trip. The winter woods were wet and slippery with fallen leaves, so they'd been told to stay on the trail for safety reasons. Of course he decided to blaze his own trail. He slipped in the leaves and careened head over heels. His downhill slide stopped at the edge of a cliff that surely would have ended his foolishness—permanently.

He did learn to heed good counsel as he grew up and spent fourteen years as a middle school counselor helping to guide kids toward the good path. All too often he saw the answer they needed in their pain and struggle, but ultimately it was their choice which path they were going to take. And more times than he'd liked, he identified with the prophet Jeremiah. "Stand in the ways and see, and ask for the old paths, where the good way is, and walk in it, and you shall find rest for your souls. But they said, 'We will not walk in it'" (Jeremiah 6:16).

Without God we lack the wisdom we need to navigate

life's challenges and temptations. But we have the wonderful counselor—the possessor of all knowledge and wisdom. He promises to teach us how to stick to the right paths in life. He'll never steer you wrong, and He's always available for consultation.

- Where is the first place you usually turn for counsel about life?

- What benefits have you experienced from consulting God's Word and praying while making important decisions or navigating confusing situations?

God, You're available for counsel at any moment. Teach me Your wisdom.

INCORRUPTIBLE

For the trumpet shall sound, and the dead shall be raised incorruptible, and we shall be changed.

1 Corinthians 15:52

"It's fire and it's crashing. . . . This is terrible. This is one of the worst catastrophes in the world. . . . Oh, the humanity." Chicago reporter Herb Morrison famously described the tragedy of the *Hindenburg* explosion that killed thirty-five people on May 6, 1937. In those days airships were filled with hydrogen because it's both a light and abundant element. But hydrogen has a potentially fatal flaw—it burns. The hydrogen atom is highly reactive. A tiny spark can cause it to bond with oxygen in a violent release of energy. Today's blimps are filled with helium, which is inert and nonflammable. Even in the laboratory, scientists haven't been able to get helium to react with anything.

Sin began its violent destruction of life in Eden. It brought decay. It brought death in this world's worst catastrophe. Oh, the humanity who would suffer from its corruption. We've all been born of a corruptible seed, one that's stained by the realities of decay, deterioration, and death.

But think of the hope brought by knowing that our God is incorruptible. He lives forever as He is, never changing form or shape. Never reacting. And there's even greater news! He invites us all into this ever-unchanging life by "being born again, not of corruptible seed, but of incorruptible, through the word of God, which lives and abides forever" (1 Peter 1:23). Be born of the Spirit, and welcome the things of God.

- What are the implications of Jesus' words to Nicodemus in John 3:6–8 in your life?

- In what ways is being born of the incorruptible seed (God's Spirit) producing incorruptible fruit in your life (2 Peter 1:3–4)?

Heavenly Father, I thank You for Jesus, who made a way for us to be born into Your spiritual kingdom.

GENEROUS

"Give, and it shall be given to you. Good measure—
pressed down, and shaken together, and running over—
shall be given by men into your bosom. For with the same
measure that you use, it shall be measured back to you."

LUKE 6:38

"Here, take mine!" I'm often humbled and amazed by my middle daughter's generous heart. She can't stand to see anyone go without or feel left out. It seems the worth of everything she owns is measured solely by its value as a gift. Her greatest joy is giving. Whether it's a hug when someone is sad or her last piece of candy, she gives it all gladly.

Jesus once shared a story about three servants. Their generous master had given each of them a large sum of money to oversee for him. Later he found that two of them had doubled his investment. "Well done, good and faithful servant," he told those two (Matthew 25:21, 23). But the third servant had buried his money and made no profit. Jesus' lesson applies to far more than money. God has generously blessed each of us with gifts that we can use in our kingdom work. Whether it's your time, your musical or teaching ability, your hospitality, or something else, are you holding back and hiding your gifts out of fear, or maybe a bit of selfishness?

Nothing is too small or insignificant to be used by God. It might take only a few moments of your time, but you could change someone's eternity.

- Who in your life would you consider to be a generous person? What values or character qualities have you noticed in them as they serve others?

- In what ways would you like to grow in being more generous with your gifts?

Lord, You have generously blessed me.
Show me the areas where I am burying
my talents and not using them for You.

MERCIFUL

He delights in mercy. He will turn again. He will have compassion on us. He will subdue our iniquities. And You will cast all their sins into the depths of the sea.

MICAH 7:18–19

Sad puppy eyes meet yours. Ribs surface under thin skin that trembles in the cold. Christmas ads often pull at our heart-strings. And we *are* moved to compassion for the forty-five seconds that images of hungry or sick children and animals distract us from the sappy Christmas movie we were enjoying. We do feel compassionate—*Oh, that's just terrible*. But mostly we don't do anything.

God's compassion, however, moves Him to act in mercy. Mercy is the active form of compassion. It's getting out of your chair and rushing over to help an elderly neighbor shovel the sidewalk after a snowfall. It's offering to babysit for a single mom, taking food to a sick family, or sponsoring that hungry child. Mercy moves to relieve the suffering of others.

God was actively compassionate toward the Israelites when they cried out to Him from their slavery in Egypt. "And the children of Israel sighed because of the bondage, and they cried. And their cry came up to God because of the bondage. And God heard their groaning, and God re-membered His covenant with Abraham, with Isaac, and with

Jacob. And God saw the children of Israel, and God had respect for them" (Exodus 2:23–25). After this, God sent Moses to lead His people out of Egypt. He heard them and came to help. And later God's mercy compelled Him to help us all by sending Jesus—because mercy moves.

- God is always merciful, but in what ways do we sometimes remove ourselves from under His mercy?
- How could you turn your compassion into practical action this week?

Lord, You didn't have to move to help us, but You did. Show me who needs mercy this week.

NEAR

"Do not fear, for I am with you. Do not be dismayed, for I am your God. I will strengthen you. Yes, I will help you. Yes, I will uphold you with My righteous right hand."

ISAIAH 41:10

The bed dipped and I glanced at the clock: 3:00 a.m. Our youngest daughter clambered over me and plopped into the middle of the bed. "I had a bad dream." She grabbed her dad's arm and held on like he was the last unicorn cupcake at the birthday party.

Suddenly, as she held on to her father, the shadows seemed less threatening. She ceased her worry and relaxed into sleep because she wasn't alone. All she needed to soothe her anxious, fearful mind during the dark hours was the knowledge that her father was right beside her. She trusted him to shield her and handle all the details she didn't understand.

Our heavenly Father is with us through every hardship and scary place. Reach out and grab His hand for comfort in the dark hours of your life. You are not alone. Talk to Him about all of your trials. He assures us, "Do not be afraid or be dismayed, for the LORD your God is with you wherever you go" (Joshua 1:9). God's presence is always a game changer.

- How do your responses to trials in life reflect or not reflect the nearness of God? What activities help you feel God's presence in your life?

- Read Philippians 4:4–7 and consider how God's nearness affects your response to life's troubles.

Heavenly Father, I often react with fear or frustration when ____________ happens. Help me to remember Your nearness and respond in faith and gentleness.

CONFIDENCE

He has said, "I will never leave you or forsake you."
So we may boldly say, "The Lord is my helper,
and I will not fear what man shall do to me."

HEBREWS 13:5–6

A tremor ran through her. A cancer diagnosis was not what she'd been expecting. Deep breath. God was in this with her. It wasn't outside His sphere of influence. And it certainly wasn't bigger than He was. She would trust Him as she always had.

She was in good company. Joseph was the epitome of calm, cool, and collected in crisis. A famine had dried the land to a desiccated husk around him. But Joseph managed Egypt's affairs flawlessly because he believed God and faithfully followed the plan God had given him. Because of this, he saved lives—including the lives of his family.

The apostle Paul wrote, "I can do all things through Christ who strengthens me" (Philippians 4:13). More confident words have never been spoken, but he wasn't working on his golf game at the country club at the time. No, Paul was in prison—and in all probability headed for his death. In good times. In bad times. In hunger or in comfort. He could do hard things because God was his confidence.

What's your crisis? The economy? Politics? A wayward child? Health problems? Finances? Divorce? In all these things "the earth is the Lord's" (Psalm 24:1). His ways are higher than our ways (Isaiah 55:9). His wisdom is deep (Romans 11:33). We can believe and be confident in God. Obey God. And endure to the end (Matthew 24:13).

- How do you normally respond in a crisis?
- In what ways does Hebrews 13:5–6 help you find confidence and calm in your crises?

Lord, I don't understand all that is happening to me, but I know that You are here with me to help me.

SHIELD

The LORD is my strength and my shield.
My heart trusted in Him, and I am helped.
PSALM 28:7

An agonized scream pierced the smoky air of the campground. I knew that scream. Fear shot down my spine like ice water. It was my daughter, and something was very wrong. I sprinted toward the ruckus. Our six-year-old had lost control of her bike while speeding down a steep hill. The crash could have been catastrophic. The side of her bike helmet was gouged by the pavement. I have never been more thankful for a polystyrene-lined piece of molded plastic. Her precious little head was safe and sound, but she did snap her collarbone cleanly in two.

Much like a little girl careening down a hill, brakes forgotten, we can feel vulnerable and exposed to a legion of attacks. Fear moves in and faith flees. Life is incredibly fragile, and we keep count of all the possibilities for disaster. But God is fiercely protective of those He loves: "You, O LORD, are a shield for me, my glory, and the lifter up of my head" (Psalm 3:3). God guards us in countless ways every day, including from the enemy. When we're in spiritual battles, He is a shield against temptation. God told Abram, "Do not fear,

Abram. I am your shield and your exceedingly great reward" (Genesis 15:1). This doesn't mean that nothing bad will ever happen to us here, but it does mean that no matter what, God is your defender who covers and protects you.

- What does Ephesians 6:16 teach us about the shield that God has given us?

- Who is the sustainer of our faith according to Hebrews 12:2, and what does this teach us about God's protection?

Lord, keep my faith strong in the midst of spiritual attacks. I am a broken sinner in need of a shield.

COMPASSION

But when He saw the multitudes, He was moved with compassion for them, because they were without hope and were scattered, like sheep having no shepherd.

MATTHEW 9:36

She must have been wrong. She'd made assumptions. She'd misjudged. She'd judged—and that was the core problem. She'd taken offense where none was meant, misread intentions, and assumed quiet aloofness was dislike. But now she knew better. Her coworker didn't have time for friends because she worked two jobs. It was difficult to pull a smile from her because she was exhausted and overwhelmed by the demands of single motherhood. And the snap in her voice stemmed from stress and anxiety.

We've all felt the sting of being misunderstood. Yet we're often ready to take every response and reaction to us personally. We become the center of our own universe, and the lives of others revolve around our perceptions and interactions with them. The Bible says that we are to bear one another's burdens. . .because of our love (Galatians 6:2). Unfortunately, too often we fail to realize that others are carrying burdens. And forget trying to understand them.

But that isn't at all what Jesus did for us. He saw our

suffering and sin, and He carried the burden of the cross to save us from it. The least we could do is help lighten another's load through understanding and compassion. Every one of us carries the impression of God's fingerprint. We are each unique and loved dearly by Him. Try to understand another person's reality and allow it to open your heart.

- Consider how you respond to your friends and family, or even a cranky waitress. How have you judged and taken offense instead of being curious about their circumstances and offering compassion?

- In what ways can you show Jesus' compassion to the world around you?

Lord, help me to see others through Your eyes of compassion.

JOY

Though now you do not see Him, yet believing, you rejoice with joy unspeakable and full of glory, receiving the result of your faith, even the salvation of your souls.
1 PETER 1:8–9

"She's almost here. You can do this!" Our first daughter was about to enter the world, but I was beginning to think this painful experience was not going to end, and I wondered if I had the strength to see it through. But incredibly, the moment they placed that little bundle in my arms, joy and love flooded into previously unexplored hollows of my heart. On one of the happiest days of my life, joy flowed easily. But all my pregnancies didn't end with a little "bundle of joy." I miscarried during our third pregnancy. And instead of happiness I was stricken with loss. I was expecting good things, but I'd gotten grief. How did joy fit with my brokenness?

Job understood suffering and loss. But in his grief he didn't shake his fist at God. No, he worshipped. "Naked I came out of my mother's womb and naked I shall return there. The LORD gave and the LORD has taken away. Blessed be the name of the LORD" (Job 1:21).

Blessed be the name of the Lord who never stops loving us, who is always in control, who is not the cause of our pain, and who soon will defeat the principalities and powers of this world that wage war against our souls! When you put your faith in God, your joy is sourced not from your current circumstances but from the one who holds all things together (Colossians 1:17).

- In light of Habakkuk 3:17–19, how can we rejoice in God during struggles?

- What is preventing you from trusting in God's sovereignty and rejoicing in the Lord?

Lord, I can always have joy because circumstances do not change who You are. Please remind me of this truth today.

ALPHA AND OMEGA

"I am Alpha and Omega, the beginning and the ending," says the Lord, "who is, and who was, and who is to come, the Almighty."

REVELATION 1:8

The trip was a disaster. The lake was horribly overcrowded, the heat was unbearable, and the kids were cranky. That evening black clouds clawed their way across the sky toward our eerily quiet campground. The air felt unnaturally still. A storm was coming. As we mapped out the distance to the nearest storm shelter, I picked up our one-year-old and realized that the severe storm warning and lack of proper shelter wasn't our only problem. She was burning with fever.

Are you dreading what tomorrow might bring because today is trending toward trials? Jesus promised that in this world we will have trouble. It never seems to fail. The Israelites went on a forty-year camping trip in the wilderness because they didn't trust God's ability to deliver them to the promised land. Even though they hadn't stuck with God, He stuck with them. No matter what troubles your journey is taking you through, God has arrived ahead of you. He is Alpha and Omega. The first and the last. Nothing came before Him, and nothing will come after Him. He knows your future, and He's already there.

Yes, we will have trials, but oh the comfort of knowing that the Alpha and the Omega—He who was first and stretches into all eternity—has already overcome the world (John 16:33). He can bring peace into this storm—for you.

- How can knowing that God is both the beginning and the end of all things give you delight about your eternal future instead of dread over tomorrow?

- Or if you do feel dread over your eternal future, what do you need to do to change that?

God, there is no place I can end up where You are not already there. Please give me a confident hope in You.

HEALER

Who Himself bore our sins in His own body on the tree, that we, being dead to sins, should live for righteousness, by whose wounds you were healed.

1 PETER 2:24

A bump on the knee, a scrape with no blood—even when they're not needed, kids believe in the magical power of Band-Aids applied by Mom with a kiss. Our kisses and bandages don't actually have the power to heal their hurts, knit their cuts back together, or erase the emotional pains they've felt, but our love makes all the difference. Through the pain of their bumps and bruises, we help them discover courage and self-control. Through their battered feelings we teach them emotional maturity and compassion for others. Through their pain the tender new shoots of growth bloom.

God knows we'll all be scraped on the sharp edges of a sin-shattered world. As the great physician, His love surrounds us, and He offers spiritual healing for all. Now. Today. He's the ultimate healer of our most deadly ailment—sin. Jesus went to the cross so that by His wounds we could be healed—healed of our irritation, impatience, criticism, and pride. Healed of our lust for pleasures, our anger, envy, and selfishness.

God is always for our growth. Dare to believe that your pain and suffering in this life can end not in despair but instead in unshakable hope: "We also glory in tribulations, knowing that tribulation works patience, and patience experience, and experience hope" (Romans 5:3–4). Our pain will always change us. Hope in a God who brings healing and growth.

- In what ways has your past suffering led you toward God or away from Him?
- How does viewing suffering as an opportunity for growth shape your view of God's goodness and love toward you?

Heavenly Father, heal me of my sin and help me to grow.

SELF-CONTROLLED

Let your moderation be known to all men.
The Lord is at hand. Be anxious for nothing.
PHILIPPIANS 4:5–6

One glance at social media or the news headlines is all you need to see that today's emotions are running hot and exploding into reckless words and violent actions. Proverbs 25:28 says, "He who has no rule over his own spirit is like a city that is broken down and without walls." Throughout history a city's walls were vital for protection. Without fortification it would be easily overrun by the enemy.

God tells us that self-control is our protective wall. It allows us to choose our path. So why do we so often allow our heightened emotions to wreck us and those we lash out at? The apostle Paul told us in Philippians that even in volatile, emotionally charged, stressed-out situations, we can choose self-control over out-of-control. Our gentleness toward others should flow from our rock-solid belief that God is near.

When we're feeling offended or crushed by life's pressure, we can respond like our imperturbable God. He doesn't get overwhelmed by emotions or stretched thin by stress. His temperament is always seasoned, mature, and steady. His love, mercy, grace, and justice are always on purpose. We can share in His calm by remembering that the sovereign God of the universe is near. And He is in control. We can release our provoking anxiety and respond to others in gentleness in every situation. Learn a new language—the language of God's love.

- In what areas of your life is your gentleness being challenged by a difficult circumstance?
- How does Philippians 4:5 instruct us to show gentleness in hard times?

Lord, please calm the chaos inside of me as You did the storms of the sea. Give me strength to choose what is good even when it's hard.

THE WAY

Jesus said to him, "I am the way,
the truth, and the life."
John 14:6

Twenty thousand words—I'm convinced my daughter's talent for talk exceeds this daily average, and most of her words come in the form of questions. One night we stopped at a Road Closed sign on a backcountry byway in unfamiliar territory. As I pondered my options, panic shook my daughter's small frame and her words wobbled out. "How will we get home?"

Jesus' disciple Thomas was a lot like my daughter. He needed the details, the plan, to ease his anxiety. On Jesus' last night with His disciples, He told them not to worry: "I go to prepare a place for you" (John 14:2). I imagine Thomas' hand shot up, but Jesus answered his question before he could ask it. "You know where I go, and you know the way" (verse 4).

Wait. What? Jesus had maddeningly left out some key information. "Lord, we do not know where You go," Thomas said, "and how can we know the way?" (verse 5). How could Jesus be calm when Thomas *needed* directions to his friend's new digs? But Jesus pointed out that Thomas was eye to eye with the answer: "I am the way, the truth, and the life. No man comes to the Father except through Me" (John 14:6).

My daughter and I made it home that night. GPS is a godsend. In the midst of his distress, Thomas just needed to recognize his Godsend, and ours. Jesus is the way—to grace in our failure, strength in our weakness, hope in our darkness. Jesus is the way home.

- Although Thomas was concerned with where Jesus was going in John 14:5–7, what was Jesus really trying to teach the disciples?

- In what ways have you experienced Jesus as "the way" in your own life?

Jesus, You are the only way to God.
May I always trust Your leading.

RESURRECTION

If we have hope in Christ only in this life, we are of all men most miserable. But now Christ has been raised from the dead and has become the firstfruits of those who have fallen asleep.
1 Corinthians 15:19–20

"They've taken Him!" Mary doubled over, chest heaving to drag air into her screaming lungs. She couldn't believe this. His death was agony, and now someone had stolen His body. Peter and John sprinted away to the tomb. Mary walked slowly back to the place where they'd laid Jesus' body. Tears burned tracks down her cheeks that mirrored the scorches on her heart. Empty. The tomb was empty. She turned to go. But then she heard "Mary." She'd heard the pull of that voice calling her name before. Her heart stuttered in her chest. "Rabboni!"

Praise God that Jesus came back from the dead in the most earth-shattering event in history. Our faith is not futile, and we are not still in our sins (1 Corinthians 15:14). Our hope for heaven is proved by His resurrection. And someday we will join Him.

"Behold, I tell you a mystery: We shall not all sleep, but we shall all be changed, in a moment, in the twinkling of an eye. . . . The dead shall be raised incorruptible, and we shall be changed. For this corruptible must put on incorruption, and this mortal must put on immortality" (1 Corinthians 15:51–53). We will drop this husk of mortality and put on immortality with Christ. The sting of death is defeated. Jesus is alive!

- How can meditating on scriptures about the resurrection help alleviate our fear of death?
- What would be the implications for our faith if Jesus had not risen from the dead?

Jesus, death could not hold You! You are Lord even over death. I can persevere because my eyes are fixed on what is to come.

SPIRIT

"God is a Spirit."
JOHN 4:24

Ebenezer Scrooge is the epitome of stingy characters and represents our dark obsession with the sparkly and distracting things of this world. It took visits from three spirits to set him free from the lie that wealth brings security and satisfaction. His dreams caused him to wake up to the reality that money couldn't buy him what he was looking for, and in fact his eternal security was at risk.

God isn't made of physical matter. Instead, as a spirit, He has the incredible ability to be with us everywhere. Jesus touched on this in an interesting conversation with a disreputable Samaritan woman. While they were discussing where people should worship, Jesus told her, "God is a Spirit, and those who worship Him must worship Him in spirit and in truth" (John 4:24). God is an invisible, incorporeal, living person. Because He is immaterial, He doesn't measure blessings by our net worth. He values the immaterial blessings of His kingdom—peace, contentment, love, joy—the meaning and purpose in life that's found in a loving relationship with Himself and others.

We tend to believe that we aren't blessed unless we have

something tangible to prove it. But God's kingdom is not of this world. Even more, as believers we have the unimaginable privilege of the Holy Spirit dwelling in us. We can worship Him anywhere because we are His temple, the place He wants to be. Wake up to the things of the Spirit and worship God in spirit and in truth.

- What changes do you need to make in your priorities in light of knowing that God is spirit?

- In what ways does knowing that you are the temple of the Holy Spirit affect your thoughts and actions?

God, how amazing that You are with me always, dwelling in me, allowing me to worship You anywhere and making a way for me to access Your kingdom.

RIGHTEOUS

That I may win Christ and be found in Him,
not having my own righteousness, which is of the
law, but that which is through the faith of Christ,
the righteousness that is of God by faith.
PHILIPPIANS 3:8–9

We simply did not have what we needed. My eight-year-old desperately wanted to take a horse project in 4-H. But we didn't have a suitable horse for showing. The answer to both her prayers and wildest dreams came in the form of a big, laid-back Appaloosa quarter horse named Jack. A friend offered him to my daughter for the summer so he wouldn't sit idle in her field. Jack was just what she needed.

We too are lacking what we need to come before God. In ourselves we don't have the required righteousness to walk into His presence—not since Eve got hungry for more than the status quo in the garden. No matter how hard we try, perfection seems so far off. But our heavenly Father, in His great compassion for us, "knows our form; He remembers that we are dust" (Psalm 103:14). And He had a plan to give us what we needed.

"As far as the east is from the west, so far has He removed our transgressions from us" through Jesus (Psalm 103:12). He gave us what we lacked—"the righteousness of God that is by faith in Jesus Christ" (Romans 3:22). Jesus never stepped wrong. He lived the perfect righteous life that we couldn't. It cost Him greatly, but He gives it freely to us. Praise God! He no longer sees our sins but instead the spotless robes of His own righteousness.

- What is the connection between faith and righteousness?
- As believers, how is it possible for us to live right before God (Romans 6:16–23)?

Lord Jesus, thank You for living the righteousness that I couldn't and dying to wash away my stains of guilt.

DWELLING PLACE

Lord, You have been our dwelling place in all generations.
Psalm 90:1

They were coming! Excitement coursed through her as she ended the call with her daughter. All of her children would be home for Thanksgiving. The rooms would once again know laughter and the hum of happy conversation. Her house had been so empty and quiet. She walked past vacant bedrooms each day and drank her coffee each morning without interruption. Her house had become a place to be. But a home was a place to belong. And soon they would all be together again.

It has always been God's plan to be with us. Ever since sin shattered the serenity of His garden, He had a rescue plan in motion. His deep love for us demands closeness—He yearns to have His children around His table. Our souls are eternal. God made them to be that way. And in the end we have a choice. Will we dwell with God eternally. . .or apart from Him because we turned down our seat at His table?

In John's vision of Revelation, a loud voice cried out from the throne, "Behold, the tabernacle of God is with men, and He will dwell with them, and they shall be His people" (Revelation 21:3). From the beginning to the end, He has always wanted to be with us. Jesus doesn't desire you for a passing acquaintance. He wants to be the place where you belong. In your laughter and tears, live each moment in Him.

- What does it mean to your spiritual life to have God as your dwelling place while living in this "not yet" world?

- In what areas of your life are you not dwelling in God?

Lord, thank You for being our dwelling place where we find peace and belonging.

MAJESTIC

"Yours, O Lord, is the greatness and the power and the glory and the victory and the majesty, for all that is in heaven and on the earth is Yours. Yours is the kingdom, O Lord, and You are exalted as head above all. Both riches and honor come from You, and You reign over all."

1 Chronicles 29:11–12

The mist hung over the water on a scarlet-streaked summer dawn. It was the perfect day for sunrise slalom skiing. The water of the mountain lake stretched smooth as a glass tabletop, undisturbed by wind or other vacationers. The mountains framed the lake in regal peaks, both stately and serene. Sitting in our small ski boat surrounded by God's stunning creation, I felt small in the presence of my great God.

God is a gloriously good king. He's enthroned in unapproachable light and pulsing with eternal power (1 Timothy 6:16). Death has no rule over Him, and He is both great and kind, imposing and attractive, powerful and gentle. He is "the Majestic One" (Isaiah 10:34 ESV).

Sometimes our sinful desires try to drag us away from His rule and convince us that He isn't good—that under His rule we will be required to give up more than we gain, and that like many earthly kings He will only take from us for His own pleasure and increase. But in Christ we gain so much. We become daughters to the High King of heaven. He wants to adopt you, bring you into His household, and give you the privileges of being His family. He alone is worthy of all your praise. Who will be your king today?

- What images come to mind when you think of God's majesty?
- What hesitations or desires are preventing you from surrendering certain areas of your life to God's rule?

God, You are robed in majesty.
Your greatness draws worship from my soul.

BREAD OF LIFE

"I am the living bread that came down from heaven. If any man eats of this bread, he shall live forever."

JOHN 6:51

The cookie jar was empty. Every year for Christmas my Italian father-in-law bakes mountains of the most deliciously addicting biscotti. But since I'd decided to purge my cupboards and eat healthier after the holidays, the divine twice-baked cookies I was craving were absent. My brain knows they have zero nutritional value, but my body still craves their anise and chocolate chip goodness. Ultimately, they always leave me feeling unsatisfied. So I eat more. You can understand my problem.

The crowds following Jesus were craving divine food too. Just the day before, Jesus had manifested a meal for more than five thousand people, and now their stomachs were empty again. But Jesus knew what they were about. "Labor not for the food that perishes but for that food that endures to everlasting life, which the Son of Man shall give to you," He told them (John 6:27). Jesus had something much more filling, more life sustaining, than mere food. He wanted them to look past their immediate desire and into eternity. "I am the bread of life," He said. "He who comes to Me shall never hunger" (John 6:35).

Come experience a life of fullness. Filled with meaning. Saturated with satisfaction. Brimming with joy and peace. All your spiritual longings to know God will be met. Abandon the empty, unsatisfying things in this life.

- What does it mean to you that Jesus is the Bread of Life? What earthly things have been your focus, and how can you shift to thinking about spiritual things?

- If Jesus, unlike bread, can satisfy us forever, what does that mean for our day-to-day living in the present?

Lord, You are everything I need. Help me to find my satisfaction in You and not in the temporary things of this earth.

UNIQUE

Who is like the Lord *our God, who dwells on high, who humbles Himself to see the things that are in heaven and on the earth? He raises up the poor out of the dust and lifts the needy out of the dunghill, that He may set him with princes, even with the princes of His people.*

Psalm 113:5–8

Snow floats down to wrap our drab winter world in white. Each tiny hexagonal crystal has been formed by its own unique experience. On January 5, 1856, Henry David Thoreau wrote in his journal: “How full of the creative genius is the air in which these are generated! I should hardly admire more if real stars fell and lodged on my coat. Nature is full of genius, full of the divinity; so that not a snowflake escapes its fashioning hand.” Each flake reflects our one-of-a-kind God.

If God cares to make the fleeting snow special, imagine how much more of Himself He’s poured into crafting your unique gifts, talents, and personality. In the snowstorm of society, no two human beings are alike. The breathtaking beauty and function of God’s people lies in the symphony of our gifts. “We have many parts in one body and all parts do not have the same function, so we, being many, are one body in Christ” (Romans 12:4–5).

But all those unique moving parts can sometimes get in a bind. Sometimes we forget the value of our differences. Instead of comparing or conforming, discover how you can serve God with your unique traits (1 Peter 4:10).

- In what ways does comparing yourself to others or being envious of their talents rob you of your purpose?

- In what ways does Jeremiah 29:11 give you acceptance and purpose in your uniqueness?

Lord, there is none like You. I thank You that I reflect my Creator in my one-of-a-kind way. Show me how to use my talents for You.

THE WORD

In the beginning was the Word, and the Word was with God, and the Word was God.

JOHN 1:1

Silence. Waiting. Jewish children were born. They grew. They waited for the Messiah to come. They went to synagogue. When white hair crowned their heads, they strained their ears for God to speak, and they promised their grandchildren that the Messiah would come. They waited a little longer. The world held its breath in anticipation. Then, when God was ready, four hundred years of His silence shattered with the squall of a swaddled infant—"the Word was made flesh and dwelled among us" (John 1:14). God—the all-powerful, all-knowing, infinite Creator—walked this earth with us again as the incarnate Word. Jesus—fully human, fully God—came to unveil God's grace and truth to a world dying of anticipation.

Jesus' disciple Philip once asked Him to show them the Father. He hadn't yet understood that God, in the flesh, had pitched His tent with them. Jesus gently replied, "Have I been with you so long, and still you have not known Me, Philip? He who has seen Me has seen the Father" (John 14:9). God's Word, the instrument of His will, showed up to show us the Father.

- To reveal Himself to us in a way that we could understand, the Word became flesh. What does this show us about God's love?

- What should our response be to the God who emptied Himself and "made Himself of no reputation and took on Himself the form of a servant and was made in the likeness of men" (Philippians 2:7)?

Father, thank You for speaking to us through Jesus. Help me to listen for Your still, small voice.

ROCK

Who is a rock except our God?
PSALM 18:31

"I am not a two-hundred-pound man!" I yelled at my husband. He looked me up and down with a grin and said, "Well, thank the Lord for that!" A laugh burst through my frustration even if we were failing to bust through this hard ground. We were digging post holes for a fence behind our barn with a two-man auger. Notice the word *man* in that description. I was severely lacking the height and muscle needed for this piece of machinery, and we'd hit hard-packed rocky soil eighteen inches into a four-foot hole. "One more try," he coaxed and fired up the engine. The corkscrew bit started to spin. We lowered it into the hole. The hard ground grabbed the bit and ripped the handles from my grip. Quicker than a chick pecks a bug, the handles whipped around and gut-punched my husband. In my defense I did try to warn him. With the help of much stronger reinforcements, that post can now hold up a horse.

Jesus said that a wise man hears His words and puts them into practice and is secure: "The rain descended, and the floods came, and the winds blew and beat on that house, and it did not fall, for it was founded on a rock" (Matthew 7:25).

But sometimes we've played the fool; we've built sandcastles because we've preferred to go our own way. And when the hardships came, our castle collapsed, "and great was its fall" (Matthew 7:27). God is a solid foundation. He's bedrock—firm and unchanging. Build your life on the solid foundation of God's Word and your faith won't falter.

- In what ways are you living your life conformed to God's Word, and in what ways are you living after the pattern of the world?

- What has God taught you through the storms you've experienced?

Lord, give me wisdom and strength to live like You.

REST

We who have believed enter into rest.
HEBREWS 4:3

Do the next thing. It was the mantra of her days. Just keep going and move on to the next thing. *Overwhelmed* was too kind a word to describe her mindset, and *exhausted* was too gentle for the harsh weariness that clouded her mind and hung on her limbs. She was struggling in survival mode.

Jesus knows about the heavy cares and burdens that life can bring. He said, "Come to Me, all you who labor and are heavy-laden, and I will give you rest. Take My yoke on you and learn from Me, for I am meek and lowly in heart, and you shall find rest for your souls. For My yoke is easy and My burden is light" (Matthew 11:28–30).

Do you need a lighter burden? Rest? You don't have to bear such heaviness. After all, the only baggage we have is what we choose to carry with us. You can drop your load of worry and stress at the feet of Jesus and pick up the peace of mind that comes with knowing that God is in control—of everything. Concerning political situations and world leaders, the increasing violence and hostile culture, inflation, your family's safety and provision—all of it is in His hands. Your days might not be less busy and your body will still tire, but your soul can be at rest.

Find comfort in God's words to Moses as the Israelites departed Sinai for the promised land: "My presence shall go with you, and I will give you rest" (Exodus 33:14). Go with God. Be at rest.

- What are the implications of God's sovereignty for our everyday lives, and how does this affect our rest?

- Read Hebrews 4:1–11. In what ways does our obedience or disobedience affect our ability to rest in God?

Lord, You are my rest. I have peace because You are with me.

COVENANT

He who promised is faithful.
HEBREWS 10:23

"Mom, you promised!" Kids tend to be firmly black-and-white in their outlook. Sure, I might have said that we'd go bowling, but I didn't foresee the flat tire in my future. Sometimes we make promises we don't intend to keep, and other times circumstances jerk the wheel out of our hands when our plans blow a tire.

The great thing about God is He's much more dependable than we are. Throughout time, even when we've thrown down our end of the bargain, God has always kept His promises. And His plans are never prevented by unforeseen breakdowns. God made covenants with Noah, Abraham, Moses, and David. Each promise kept brought Him closer to restoring His relationship with the people He loves.

Finally, our great covenant-keeping God stepped even closer. Jesus said, "This is My blood of the new covenant, which is shed for many for the remission of sins" (Matthew 26:28). He forgave our sins, put His Spirit in us, and turned our stony hearts into flesh. Then He gave us a new way of worship—one that was no longer written on the unyielding tablets of stone but written on our hearts (Jeremiah 31:31–34). Praise God that He never goes back on His word.

- When you reflect on God's covenant-keeping character and promises, how are you moved to hope?

- Read Ezekiel 36:26–27. How is the new covenant better? Which promises are comforting or convicting to you right now?

Lord, You are the great promise keeper. You have filled me with Your Spirit and given me a new heart. Help me to follow You faithfully.

OMNIPOTENT

"With men this is impossible,
but with God all things are possible."
MATTHEW 19:26

"How will this be?" Mary's question echoed Zechariah's words to the angel Gabriel six months earlier in the temple. But in stark contrast to the priest's doubt, the words of this young, unwed Jewish girl were drenched in her belief that God could do what He said He would. When given the fantastic news that she was favored by God and would soon have a baby—and not just any baby but Immanuel, a son who would be called the Son of the Most High God—she didn't doubt God. "Behold the handmaid of the Lord," she said. "May it be to me according to your word" (Luke 1:38).

Gabriel had told her, "With God nothing shall be impossible" (Luke 1:37). His power has neither borders nor blackouts. Mary trusted in God's absolute and complete power in her situation because she knew the God of scripture. Her belief became a song of praise: "He who is mighty has done great things for me, and holy is His name" (Luke 1:49). She knew it was inevitable that the kingdom of heaven would come, just as He'd said. Mary's weakness met God's strength, and the miraculous occurred.

In His magnificent power God gave us more than we were hoping for, more than we imagined possible. Instead of a mere sovereign, He sent a Savior. Have you slammed into a situation that seems beyond repair? Believe, like Mary, with the humble heart of a servant, and His strength will be made perfect in your weakness (2 Corinthians 12:9).

- What truth about God's omnipotence do you struggle to believe?
- What might change in your life if you responded with a posture of trust in His power and a servant's heart instead of doubt?

Heavenly Father, help me to trust that Your strength fills all the gaps of my weakness.

UNCHANGING

"Of old You have laid the foundation of the earth, and the heavens are the work of Your hands. They shall perish, but You shall endure. Yes, all of them shall grow old like a garment; as a garment You shall change them, and they shall be changed, but You are the same, and Your years shall have no end."

Psalm 102:25–27

"Could you please make this work?" Exasperated, I hand my phone to my daughter. Technology continually leaves me choking in its dust. At some point I'll probably become frozen in whatever decade I step off the technology train. Too many rapid changes leave me with a twinge of anxiety and a longing for the familiar.

Eve probably felt the same longing for the good old days, before sin crashed her life and changed everything. How many times she must have revisited that moment in her mind—and wished for a different outcome.

Some of us fear change and some of us embrace it. Some of us are okay with change as long as it's a change we like. Eve's circumstances changed for the worse; maybe your life has taken a left turn you'd rather have avoided. But God remains unaltered through every edition of your daily life. His goodness, mercy, justice, grace, love—all are unchanging through the ages. The same God who spoke a universe into being is the unchanging constant who gives us peace and hope in our future with Him.

- Do you usually embrace change or fear it? What major life changes have happened to you recently, and how did you view them?

- How does the knowledge of God's unchanging character help you find strength and courage when life feels uncertain?

Lord, changes can be both exhilarating and scary.
But Your love for me is always the same.

KNOWABLE

"You shall seek Me and find Me,
when you search for Me with all your heart."
JEREMIAH 29:13

Her wall was lined with diplomas marking a lifetime of acquired knowledge. And yet she still felt baffled by her existence, mortality, and her emptiness despite all her accomplishments. She saw now that she'd been deceived by a dead end.

Are you seeking something greater than yourself, something to help you make sense of life? Because God created us, we have an inner longing to know Him. He put it there and shaped it so that nothing in this world could fill it except Him. You can know God. He came here to earth. Jesus is "the image of the invisible God" (Colossians 1:15). He said, "He who has seen Me has seen the Father" (John 14:9).

Your story doesn't have to be one of a dissatisfying life. Jesus asked His would-be followers, "What are you seeking?" He asks us the same. If you're looking for purpose, forgiveness, and a place to belong, Jesus invites you to come and see who God is. Come and see for yourself what He has done for you. Come and see what He is still doing. God is the only salve that will soothe your inner strife. Look into the face of your Savior, Jesus, and you will look into the face of the God who promises us life more abundant (John 10:10).

- What do you know about God?
- How can we be deceived by our own image of God? Does your impression of what God is like line up with who the Bible says Jesus is? What adjustments might you need to make?

God, You are both incomprehensible and knowable. I'm forever grateful that You sent Jesus to show us who You are. Give me the strength to follow Him until the end.

INFINITE

Before the mountains were brought forth or
You had ever formed the earth and the world,
even from everlasting to everlasting, You are God.
Psalm 90:2

Salty. Smoky. Perfection. My teeth sank into the thin caramelized crust, exposing the pink fibers of exquisitely tender beef. My husband makes a mean steak. But unfortunately, where the grill ends, so do his skills in the kitchen. Boiled-over pasta and scorched pots are his signature dishes. If it doesn't involve searing meat on hot metal, he's going to mince you a hot mess.

Although our limits are exposed by our many failures—from culinary crashes to wrecked relationships—God doesn't suffer from our shortcomings. He's infinite in every way. It's hard to fathom an infinite God because our world is defined by limits. We have limited resources, limited time, limited patience, and limited skills. We live by speed limits, property lines, and deadlines. But pick a number and start adding zeros. Keep doing that for a few hundred years, and you won't even begin to approach infinite. God is more than that.

Life will always have struggles, but God is more. The God who has no end and no beginning is bound by nothing but

His good character. And He will keep His promise that after we have suffered for a little while He will restore, confirm, strengthen, and establish us (1 Peter 5:10).

God's infinite nature also means that He's more for your life. More love. More peace. More joy. More strength. More truth. Jesus is the shattering of your ending point as He draws you, the finite human, into eternity with Him.

- What are some limits you tend to push?

- Psalm 90 lists many of our human limitations. In what ways does it answer these limitations with God's infiniteness?

Lord, my life is limited in so many ways, but I know You are infinite. Give me great confidence in Your infinite nature.

CONSISTENT

"I am the Lord*; I do not change."*
Malachi 3:6

A decade of hard work, weekends, and staying after hours had finally culminated in a dead end. She shut her office door with more force than necessary and plopped into her chair. Fury and despair played a cruel tug-of-war with her emotions as the heavy realization settled into her bones: she'd wasted a decade of her career in a dead-end job. Her boss was both biased and inconsistent. He'd failed to credit her for her work, and she'd been passed over for a promotion—again.

Praise God that He doesn't say one thing and do another. He is both good and powerful. We can trust in God and experience His peace in the midst of an uncertain world because we know that He never changes. He is constant in His love, faithfulness, power, forgiveness, and commitment to keeping His promises (James 1:17). God is not like us.

I am an inconstant person. I'm inconsistently loving, sometimes kind, and often not as generous as I could be. Scripture says, "A double-minded man is unstable in all his ways" (James 1:8). Instead of us living torn between God and the world with our minds tossed about like a stormy sea, Paul said to "let this mind be in you, which was also in Christ

Jesus" (Philippians 2:5). Think like Jesus, with the humble and obedient mindset of a servant of God, and you'll experience more consistency in life.

- In what ways does the fact that God's promises never change affect your ability to trust Him?
- What is your reaction to people with fickle emotions and mood swings? How does knowing that God is constant in His mood and feelings encourage you to approach Him with the difficulties, needs, and joys of life?

Heavenly Father, I find great comfort in knowing that You never change. Give me the mind of Christ and help me to act as He would.

I AM

"I Am has sent me to you."
Exodus 3:14

Barefoot, Moses stood on holy ground to meet Yahweh. God said, "I Am": I am the unchanging, uncreated, all-powerful, all-knowing, faithful, and loving God—the one who is the same yesterday, today, and forever. God paved the way for Moses to walk out of Egypt with around two million Israelites, cattle and sheep, gold, silver, and clothing. "They plundered the Egyptians" (Exodus 12:36 esv). God was all they needed to walk out of slavery.

Later Jesus introduced us to God by the same name—"I am": I am the bread of life who satisfies your soul's longings. I am the light of the world who takes away your blindness and guides your steps. I am the door of the sheep, the one way to your eternal home in heaven. I am the good shepherd who loves you and lays down His life for you. I am the resurrection and the life, the power over death. I am the way, the truth, and the life. I am the true vine you should abide in who gives you good fruit. Apart from Jesus we can do nothing, but in Him we discover all we need.

When Judas came with the temple police to arrest Him, Jesus asked them who they were looking for. They said,

"Jesus of Nazareth." Jesus answered them, "I Am." Yahweh. The force of His name drove them to their knees, because just as Moses had, they were standing on holy ground.

He is. Period. He always has been. And He always will be. And He says to you, "I am everything you need."

- In what areas of your life have you been trying to find fulfillment and satisfaction outside Jesus?
- What "I am" statement of Jesus is most meaningful to you and why?

Lord, You are all I need in this life and eternity. Remind me of this truth every moment!

YEARNING FOR US

I am my beloved's, and his desire is for me.
Song of Solomon 7:10

"Ow, what was that for?" Her new husband rubbed the shin she'd just kicked under the table. She considered him with narrowed eyes before she raised one brow and tipped her head toward the flirty waitress who'd just left their table. He raised his hands in surrender. "I wasn't looking. I promise. You know you're the only one I want."

God doesn't want to share your affections, either. He delights in you and yearns for you to worship Him and no other. He jealously wants more than just your heart. He yearns for you to give yourself to Him heart, mind, soul, and strength—everything that you are (Mark 12:30). Beloved, become the beautiful bride awaiting her bridegroom as you grow in faith, obedience, and love. "I am my beloved's, and my beloved is mine" (Song of Solomon 6:3).

I leave you with the apostle John's rich and tender encouragement to follow God with impassioned devotion: "We know that we are of God, and the whole world lies in wickedness. And we know that the Son of God has come and has given us an understanding, that we may know Him who is true. And we are in Him who is true, even in His Son,

Jesus Christ. This is the true God and eternal life. Little children, keep yourselves from idols" (1 John 5:19–21).

- What things are stealing your affection from God?
- In what ways does God's jealous yearning that you love, worship, and obey only Him help you when remaining faithful to Him is difficult?

God, You desire all of me. Search my life and show me anything that would take my heart from You.